A Feminist Perspective
in the Academy

A FEMINIST PERSPECTIVE IN THE ACADEMY:

The Difference It Makes

Edited by

ELIZABETH LANGLAND
WALTER GOVE

The University of Chicago Press
Chicago and London

The essays in this volume originally appeared in the Winter 1981 issue of *Soundings: An Interdisciplinary Journal* (volume 64, number 4) and are reprinted by arrangement.

The University of Chicago Press, Chicago 60637
The University of Chicago Press, Ltd., London

90 89 88 87 86 85 84 83   1 2 3 4 5

Library of Congress Cataloging in Publication Data

Main entry under title:

A Feminist perspective in the academy.

Originally issued as a special issue of Soundings, v. 64, no. 4, winter 1981.

Contents: The difference it makes / Patricia Meyer Spacks — New directions for feminist criticism in theatre and the related arts / Nancy S. Reinhardt — The feminist critique in religious studies / Rosemary Radford Ruether — [etc.]
1. Women's studies — United States.   2. Women college teachers — United States.   I. Langland, Elizabeth.   II. Gove, Walter R.   III. Soundings (New Haven, Conn.)
HQ1181.U5F45   1983   305.4′07′1173   82–17520
ISBN 0–226–46874–7 (hard)
ISBN 0–226–46875–5 (pbk.)

Contents

ACKNOWLEDGMENTS

The editors thank The Ethel Mae Wilson Fund of the Graduate School of Vanderbilt University, and the Fund's administrator Dean Ernest Q. Campbell, for sponsoring and funding the lecture series which gave rise to *A Feminist Perspective in the Academy*. The Ethel Mae Wilson Fund also assisted in defraying the cost of publication in *Soundings*.

Gratitude is likewise expressed to The Women's Studies Committee of the College of Arts and Science at Vanderbilt University for its support of the lecture series.

EDITORS' NOTES

The advent of women's studies has brought a feminist perspective into the academy—but has it made a difference there? That was the question we posed to the nine distinguished scholars who lectured at Vanderbilt in 1980–81 and who subsequently revised their lectures for publication in this volume. Has the feminist perspective transformed our curriculum; has it reshaped our materials; has it altered our knowledge? We found that feminist analyses have begun to alter scholarship, but women's studies has yet to have a substantial influence on the traditional curriculum, principally because such analyses challenge fundamental assumptions in each discipline.

A feminist perspective has made some difference to literary criticism, argues Patricia Meyer Spacks in "The Difference It Makes." In considering Jane Austen, for example, Spacks notes that it is no longer possible for a serious scholar to ignore the insights of feminist critics into Austen's novels. Yet while scholars must modify their papers in response to feminist insights, feminist scholarship appears as footnotes to articles in prestigious journals, and it rarely appears as an article in its own right, as Spacks' informal survey of such journals indicates. Furthermore, scholars often do not bring feminist scholarship into the classroom. Spacks concludes that feminist perspectives in literature are beginning to make themselves felt, but they have yet to restructure study within the discipline.

Rosemary Ruether, in her survey of religious studies, recognizes that the change there is also coming slowly. Ruether observes that women are entering seminaries in increasing numbers, but not all of them bring a feminist perspective into their ministry, and those who do tend to find themselves isolated. Seminaries still consign feminist studies to the peripheries of theological training. Looking at the drama, Nancy Reinhardt finds a similar phenomenon. Once excluded, women have now acted in the theatre, but their significance as scholars analyzing the discipline of drama remains surprisingly minimal. As

1

Ruether and Reinhardt show, one can be an important actor in a medium without necessarily challenging inherent sexist biases.

Men as well as women can hold a feminist perspective, as Carl Degler reveals in his essay, "What the Women's Movement Has Done to American History." Degler has found his scholarship enriched by the understanding and insights that have emerged as historians have paid increasing attention to women. Yet, Degler remains rare among male scholars in acknowledging that this broadening of perspectives substantially enhances our understanding of historical study and of history itself.

In the social sciences — psychology, sociology, and anthopology — our authors have pointed out some of the ways in which seemingly objective and value-free inquiry has been biased by unanalyzed assumptions about men and women. Cynthia Epstein singles out several areas of sociological research in which a feminist perspective has made researchers more sensitive to the ways they frame questions and carry out their inquiry. Janet Spence concentrates on the conceptions of masculinity and femininity used in psychology, and she documents the significant changes in our understanding of these concepts that stem from insights developed in the research of feminist psychologists. Judith Shapiro makes a distinction vital for anthropologists, who have long been sensitive to differences in male and female behavior. She cautions us to distinguish sex from gender, and she encourages anthropological researchers to examine the ways in which the development of the sexes is shaped by a culture's gender expectations. But in general, sensitivity to these issues is just beginning. And, according to Nancy Barrett's analysis of economics, and Nannerl Keohane's of political science, there is little evidence that a feminist perspective has made itself felt at all in these two disciplines.

While these nine scholars agree that a feminist perspective has begun to affect the shape of what is known — and knowable — in their respective disciplines, perhaps the more urgent note in each essay is the failure of women's studies to alter college and university curricula. Paper after paper concludes that, while the potential power to transform the disciplines is great, women's studies has not yet significantly unleashed that power. Why should this be true? Rosemary Ruether, dealing with religion's myths of our human condition, and Nancy Reinhardt, discussing drama, which since antiquity has likewise generated statements descriptive of our position in the universe, point out that women's studies has had so little impact on traditional bodies of knowledge because it challenges deeply held, often sacred beliefs, beliefs that are rooted in emotions and expressed in primitive imagery. Women's studies challenges vested interests; it uproots perspectives which are familiar, and, because familiar, comfortable.

As we consider the curriculum, we see throughout the papers that women's studies is a challenge to the status quo. As Judith Shapiro aptly observes in "Anthropology and the Study of Gender," "The emergence of women's studies programs is . . . a reflection of the extent to which the apparently unmarked courses in the academic curriculum constitute a de facto men's studies program." Male experiences and the perspectives that derive from them have traditionally defined the normative in the academic curriculum; female experience, when it has appeared at all, has been treated as inferior, irrelevant, insignificant, or even aberrant. The study of women from a feminist perspective denies such assumptions. Patricia Meyer Spacks quotes Annette Barnes's definition of feminists—a definition to which we would subscribe in this volume: "all feminists, I argue, would agree that women are not automatically or necessarily inferior to men, that role models for females and males in the current Western societies are inadequate, that equal rights for women are necessary, that it is unclear what by nature either men or women are, that it is a matter for empirical investigation to ascertain what differences follow from the obvious physiological ones, that in these empirical investigations the hypotheses one employs are themselves open to question, revision, or replacement." A feminist perspective, whether it is present in women's studies courses or in scholarly essays such as those in this volume, seeks to correct the bias present in our academic disciplines by uncovering and questioning the hidden assumptions about men and women that have shaped and informed standard academic subjects.

The fact that our understanding of Homo sapiens has incorporated the perspective of only half of the human race makes it clear that women's studies is not an additional knowledge merely to be tacked on to the curriculum. It is, instead, a body of knowledge that is *perspective transforming* and should therefore transform the existing curriculum from within and revise received notions of what constitutes an "objective" or "normative" perspective.

That women's studies should transform existing knowledge can hardly surprise us. Throughout history, "knowledge" has constantly changed in response to new understanding. Carl Degler remarks, "Although most people seem to think of the past as fixed and unchanging, much like a landscape, historians are more likely to see it as a seascape in which the scene is constantly changing and shifting." Were we to substitute for "the past" the word "knowledge," we would generate an image for the transformation of the curriculum as well—a dynamic seascape rather than a relatively static landscape. The insights and revelations that women's studies has to offer will utterly change the seascape of the academy.

To begin to take women seriously entails a radical transformation of our lives—in Ruether's words, " a radical reconstruction of the normative tradition." Just as Gulliver was lusus naturae—a freak of nature to the Lilliputians—so women and their perspectives have been lusus naturae to male-conceived academic disciplines. Cynthia Epstein, sociologist, notes that behavior in the male "in-group" is evaluated differently than similar behavior in the female "out-group." Actions deemed properly assertive in a man are, in a woman (or lusus naturae), judged aggressive and/or hostile. Psychologist Janet Spence observes that traits ascribed to "effective" individuals (sex unspecified) are the same traits people will ascribe to males and are distinct from the traits ascribed to females. The quality of effectiveness is, in short, appropriated by the masculine ideal, and to the feminine is relegated the quality of ineffectiveness.

From political science, Nannerl Keohane brings the discovery that silence is the supreme virtue for a woman: "the less heard of her, the more virtuous she must have been." The woman who has protested her inequality, her status as an outsider, may expect criticism for having used her voice—an unfeminine, aggressive act. This has been the ultimate trap for woman: she can be praised only for her silence, so she remains largely unknown, or, if known, known only through male report. Voiceless, woman is virtuous and worthy *only* if she has no reputation. And so known — or rather unknown except by report — she has remained unstudied, unexamined.

Nancy Barrett states an economic basis for these observations:

women are valued less than men. She concludes that "economic" theories have completely failed to explain sexual discrimination in the market place. Since the rational economic model does not explain sexual discrimination, it must stem from a deeply held, "normative" belief in women's inferiority.

A further question arises: Why, in an area of human endeavor that is devoted to the exploration of new ideas, has the male-normative perspective been so dearly and enduringly held? Perhaps Virginia Woolf's portrait of Prof. von X provides an answer. This satirical sketch picture, from *A Room of One's Own*, shows the Professor "engaged in writing his monumental work, *The Mental, Moral, and Physical Inferiority of the Female Sex.* . . . His expression suggested that he was labouring under some emotion that made him jab his pen on the paper as if he were killing some noxious insect as he wrote, but even when he had killed it that did not satisfy him; he must go on killing it; and even so, some cause for anger and irritation remained." Why are the "professors" angry? Woolf's answer is that the perception of female inferiority stems from man's need to feel superior, to instill confidence in himself. Any "infringement of [man's] power to believe in himself" brings anger. "Women have served all these centuries as looking-glasses possessing the magic and delicious power of reflecting the figure of man at twice its natural size," she concludes.

Woolf was writing of women and fiction. But she could have been talking about women and political science, women and sociology, women and psychology, women and religious studies, women and history. The female perspective challenges the established male-dominated curriculum, a curriculum that has served to give importance to the activities of the gender that customarily produced, defined, and transmitted it. As the voice of the "outsider" in academics, women's studies upsets this received wisdom by insisting on the importance of women's experience.

The editors of this volume could not have predicted what these several essays would say and particularly whether they would have a common thread. One emerged. It is an insistence that women matter. Women are not inferior; they are equal. They can no longer be ignored or excluded from the humanist tradition. And from this thread a clear message emerges: we cannot place women's studies off in a corner. To do so is to continue to agree implicitly that women and women's experience are tangential.

Women and women's experience are fundamental to the development and vitality of every discipline. As each discipline begins the urgent task of including women's studies within its perspectives, it aids the transformation of the whole seascape of knowledge. This second theme emerged from these essays: the study of women in any one discipline affects all of academia. In Nancy Barrett's words, "Women's studies should continue to be an interdisciplinary activity, precisely because the study of women's place through the perspective of any one discipline is likely to lead squarely into another." We believe the essays gathered here add strength to that statement; women's studies *will* continue to be interdisciplinary because the perspectives of one discipline *do* lead squarely into another. For this reason it is singularly appropriate that these essays are appearing in SOUNDINGS: An *Interdisciplinary* Journal.

We began our lecture series in 1980-81 by asking how women's studies has restructured disciplines. Many of our essayists said that, as yet, it has not. But what emerged overall was the strong and urgent message that it must. It is clear that the need for a fresh perspective, one marked by female insight and experience, has been widely perceived and that work is going forward to make women's studies an integral part of the curriculum and an agent for the transformation of human knowledge.

ELIZABETH LANGLAND
WALTER GOVE

THE DIFFERENCE IT MAKES

PATRICIA MEYER SPACKS

JANE AUSTEN USED TO LOOK a little thin, a little shrunken. She ignored the Napoleonic Wars, it was said, reproachfully; she dealt only with female — that is, trivial — concerns; she might be an important English writer, but certainly not an important *world* writer. Hardly more than half a century ago, H.W. Garrod wrote — after commenting that he found something ludicrous in the very idea of a "great woman" — "It would be difficult to name a writer of similar eminence who possessed so little knowledge of literature and history, whose experience of life was so narrowly and so contentedly confined, whose interests were at once so acute and so small, whose ideals were so irredeemably humdrum." He goes on to comment on "the monotonously subdued pitch of her ethical standards."[1]

Critics of Austen no longer sound that way. Now, on the contrary, we encounter sentences like this: "In her attention to the anonymous sex, and in her articulation of the feminine ethos, Jane Austen was as revolutionary in her own way as Mary Wollstonecraft."[2] And like this: "Although Austen clearly escapes the House of Prose that confines her heroines by making her story out of their renunciation of story-telling, she also dwells in . . . freer prospects . . . by identifying not only with her model heroines, but also with less obvious, nastier, more resilient and energetic female characters who enact her rebellious dissent from her culture, a dissent . . . only partially obscured by . . . her plot."[3] Both statements evoke a powerful, ambitious novelist quite different from the genteel spinster earlier imagined. Both statements, unsurprisingly, issue from the pens of feminist critics.

What difference has feminist criticism made? How much does

Patricia Meyer Spacks, Professor of English at Yale, is the author of many books and articles, including *The Female Imagination* and, most recently, *The Adolescent Idea: Myths of Youth and the Adult Imagination.*

7

it matter what one woman says about another, or, for that matter, about a man, even in print? Do woman critics still seem to men, as women preachers seemed to Dr. Johnson, like dogs walking on their hind legs? I think the answers to these questions are fairly hopeful: that feminist criticism has made a difference and can make more, that what women say does matter, that people who find it ludicrous for a female to declare herself a critic more often than not now keep their mouths shut. I propose to explain why I think so—it involves indirect, impressionistic, and ambiguous evidence—and also to suggest some problems that may blunt the impact of this new critical weapon.

The critics I quoted earlier on Jane Austen were women writing about a woman, but they make it difficult for men writing about that woman ever to sound quite the same again. A man may still find Austen trivial and confined—I occasionally meet, always with astonishment, someone who confides that opinion to me—but in order to say so in print, he will have to take account of such critics as Sandra Gilbert and Susan Gubar, the source of one of my quotations, and Julia Prewitt Brown, author of the other. These critics make powerful claims. Even the most forceful critical statement can be ignored, to be sure, but the more such statements multiply, the harder they are to shove out of the way. And feminist criticism has multiplied, expanding its scope and its claims in the past few years. Of course feminists can and do disagree with one another. By now one can find a body of criticism suggesting Austen's revolutionary implications, and other works, equally feminist in orientation, complaining about her compromises with convention. In all its diversity, though, feminist criticism assumes Austen's importance and assumes that it has something to do with her ways of treating women as subjects. In the light of such criticism, it becomes almost impossible simply to dismiss Austen. The critic who would do so must first engage in battle.

Feminist criticism, in other words, has provoked new debates: arguably the most important contribution any critical mode can make. Few literary commentators any longer believe—if, indeed, they ever did—that they have it in their power to proclaim definitive truth about a text. We believe now in the multiplicity of interpretation; most students of literature think that the richness, the multifariousness, the ambiguity of texts make them compelling. The great poem or novel or play defies definitive statement by being unalterably its unsummarizable self. Critics illuminate aspects of texts; they choose the aspects they will illuminate. Feminist critics, by raising new questions, have brought unexpected shapes out of the shadows. Why does it matter, they ask, that this work issues from a female mind, that a woman holds the pen? What does the book tell us about women in general, about women in a particular period, about its author's fantasies about women? How does its telling reflect particular social realities? In a volume of essays on feminist criticism published in 1977, Annette Barnes offers a definition of the feminist as part of her effort to describe the special point of view such a being brings to the critical act. Her definition deserves attention: "all feminists, I argue, would agree that women are not automatically or necessarily inferior to men, that role models for females and males in the current Western societies are inadequate, that equal rights for women are necessary, that it is unclear what by nature either men or women are, that it is a matter for empirical investigation to ascertain what differences follow from the obvious physiological ones, that in these empirical investigations the hypotheses one employs are themselves open to question, revision, or replacement."[4] Such a set of social, psychological, and physiological assumptions implies a special angle of vision—the angle from which new questions and new debates emerge.

Never before in history have so many people declared so loudly that women *matter*. Here is the fundamental ground for debate: these new questions and new points of view all imply the significance of women as selves, not merely others, and for many people, men and women, that is a disturbing idea. I went to China last spring, with a group of twenty-five professional women. We caused quite a lot of trouble, one way and another, by our endless and diverse demands. On the last day, one of our women guides made a little farewell speech. "When I first met you," she said, "I thought you were very strange and dangerous. But then I came to realize that you're all educated women, and that's why you have so many different opinions and interests. And now I feel that my mind has been made rich by you." Not everyone makes the same transition. To perceive as "strange and dangerous" the questions women are asking, even in so innocuous an area of study as English literature, is perhaps an appropriate initial response for many people who may feel threatened by the implications of these new ideas. But our guide's final comment is equally appropriate: those strange and dangerous questions contain the potential of enrichment. They have already enriched literary study, both in themselves and in the opposition they provoke.

Yet feminist criticism, for all its richness and its capacity for enrichment, can remain, in many contexts, virtually invisible. In some ways it is conspicuous. Think of the books and articles being written now that would have been unimaginable two decades ago: books on female friendships in fiction, on mothers and daughters in literature, on the history of novels by women, on women's poetry, on women's autobiographies. On the other hand, as I started to brood about how feminist thought has affected criticism, I decided to take a look at the journals in my field, not feminist journals, but periodicals devoted to literary investigation, to see what kind of mark feminist criticism had made. I didn't attempt a systematic formal investigation; I merely took the top magazine from each pile on the shelves of the Yale library's periodical room. I looked at twenty-eight journals, containing, at a conservative estimate, probably 150 articles and at least 300 reviews. (One magazine alone provided sixty-six reviews.) I found a total of three articles and two reviews manifesting a feminist perspective or considering a feminist text. The periodical with sixty-six reviews offered not the slightest indication that feminism existed as a fact of critical life.

My findings may be a fluke. One journal with no articles involving women or women's issues advertised future offerings on Joan Didion, Margaret Drabble, Gail Godwin, and Margaret Atwood; another promised a Virginia Woolf issue. I expect all the editors of all the journals would claim that they publish feminist criticism if it's good enough, and I expect the claim is true—but that the criticism has to be very good indeed, good enough to impress itself on minds of dramatically different orientation.

The three essays that found their way to print, in my random sample, *are* good, and good in a special way. All three, despite radical differences in tone and strategy, share a concern with the relation of art to life. They deal with texts from Mary Shelley's *Frankenstein* to Margaret Drabble's *The Waterfall,* uncovering social and psychological implications of women's fiction. To contemplate a text with a mind aware of inequalities in the female situation, of perplexities about the nature of male and female, of difficulties in every conceivable mode of understanding those natures—to confront a work of literature with a mind so imbued—forces the critic to make connections between the actual conditions women inhabit and their fictional habitations, between the fact of the text and the fact of its writing. Making such connections, feminist criticism insists on the primary human relevance of literature.

Unlike Marxist or psychoanalytic or structuralist criticism, feminist criticism need not (although it *may*) rest on a set of doctrines: only on a group of assumptions, such as those I specified earlier—assumptions implying perspectives, implying questions. In fact, feminist criticism can be at the same time Marxist or psychoanalytic or whatever. It commits its practitioner to passionate concerns but not to specific methodology. Its flexibility gives it strength; so, more importantly, does the power of its commitment: a power capable of disturbing some who encounter it while heartening others. This fact, I think, accounts for the peculiar intensity with which feminist criticism is attacked: such commitment constitutes a challenge. The feminist who turns her or his attention to literature says loudly that literature matters—literature as well as women—and that it matters specifically because of its relation to actuality. Moreover, feminist criticism demonstrates forcefully that other critical modes have ignored large hunks of actuality conspicuously related to the kinds of human conflict and human feeling that provide raw material for imaginative literature. At its best, feminist criticism is difficult to refute. I find it hard to imagine, for example, what an unreconstructed male chauvinist professor, if such there be, could do with Mary Poovey's essay on *Frankenstein* in *PMLA*,[5] one of the three pieces I mentioned earlier. Based on impeccable scholarship, quiet and logical, building a careful case on textual evidence, the article demonstrates—without ever saying it—that no one has thought about what Romantic ideas of imagination might have meant to women, how a woman's sensibility would change and use them. My hypothetical chauvinist might flatly say it's wrong, but he could not easily prove this. He would be hard put to patronize the essay, printed in a prestigious journal, conforming to orthodox academic standards. What's wrong with it, from his imagined point of view, is only *its* point of view, that perspective which solidifies the invisible into recognizable shapes. Some might prefer that the new insights recede quietly into the shadows, but they are out in the open now, critical facts to be reckoned with: the world will never be quite the same again.

On the other hand, feminist criticism isn't always at its best. It doesn't yet have as much impact as it might on the profession of literary study, partly because of the antagonism it arouses, partly because it has not yet fully evolved as a critical mode. The strengths I have mentioned—methodological flexibility, passionate commitment, insistence on relating art to life—imply corresponding weaknesses. Flexibility can lead to lack of discipline, to self-indulgence. The standards aren't clear yet for feminist criticism, not even the *value* of standards is clear. Critics working in a new mode want to rescue undiscovered and undervalued texts, writing in private rather than public modes, for example, like diaries and letters by undereducated women. Traditional standards of literary judgment obviously don't apply to such works; when they are imposed, the works simply disappear. So feminist criticism needs new criteria. Sometimes this perception leads to a drastic solution: not *new* criteria, but *no* criteria other than authorship by a woman. The enthusiasm with which feminists have greeted the emerging masses of previously hidden material occasionally becomes uncritical. We object to the patriarchal standards which have made us invisible; we haven't yet evolved clear non-patriarchal ones. The apparent lack of rigor in feminist procedures, the tendency toward wholesale acceptance, may make feminist critical claims sound dismissible.

The passionate commitment which underlies the best feminist criticism also sometimes supports the worst. Such commitment can confuse critical and political activity. Politics is the science of power; women feel their lack of public power and the need to claim more. Criticism enables them to make claims, enlarging their territory by insisting on new ways of reading old texts as well as the importance of reading new texts. But if the wish for power alone appears to motivate such insistence, the critical claim loses its authority.

The other side of the desire for power is the sense of privation which women have come to feel, and to encourage one another to feel. New investigations in recent years have uncovered various modes of female victimization and have made men and women alike—many men and women—increasingly conscious of the phenomenon. All enlargement of consciousness is a good thing. But the discovery of victimization can have disastrous intellectual consequences. It produces on occasion a kind of one-note criticism. Readers newly aware of the injustices perpetrated on one sex find evidence of such injustice everywhere—and, sometimes, *only* evidence of this sort. They discover over and over, in language, structure, and theme, testimony to women's victimization. When their articles are rejected by major publications, they have new evidence, direct personal evidence, of the same thing. They know that men have controlled the very language we use, and they find that women cannot escape the distortions of male language. As their discoveries multiply, yet no one seems to pay attention, they sound increasingly shrill, increasingly desperate—and then they too can be readily dismissed. As Mary Ellman pointed out quite a while ago, a favorite device for ignoring women writers is to label them "shrill." There's a neat double bind here: writers who feel neglected make more and more noise, then find themselves deprecated for making it.

Attention to the ways in which literature reflects life also creates vulnerabilities in feminist criticism. It can encourage practitioners to make texts into pretexts for expounding personal predilections or personal grievances; it can appear to trivialize the critical enterprise. Because the standards to which feminist criticism holds itself are no better defined than those by which it judges literary texts, concentration on a work's reference to actuality may cause the work itself to be forgotten, or to appear to be forgotten, in favor of reflection on the realm outside the written word. Focusing beyond the literary, such criticism runs the danger of being considered less than serious.

But let me repeat: these aspects of feminist criticism also represent its strengths. At every point, it seems to me, the strengths and the weaknesses of this new approach are closely intertwined.

Of course, as you may have noticed, I haven't said yet what feminist criticism *is*. That's another problem: no one quite knows. Annette Kolodny pointed out in a 1975 essay that feminists and their opponents share confusion about what the term implies.[6] Does it designate any criticism written by a woman? Any account of a man's book dominated or dictated by feminist political conceptions? Any treatment of any work by a woman?

I'll venture my own definition: I take feminist criticism to include any mode that approaches a text with primary concern for the nature of female experience in it—the fictional experience of characters, the deducible or imaginable experience of an author, the experience implicit in language or structure. This is a very broad definition, and by no means a universally accepted one. The absence of agreement on this point suggests another area of vulnerability. Lacking forceful, repeated articulations of what it means, what it stands for, and what it can do that no other method can achieve, feminist criticism will not readily be taken as seriously as competing modes.

Possibly that doesn't matter, or doesn't matter as much as one might suppose. Recent speculations about the nature of women's writing and women's language, as opposed to men's, have repeatedly suggested the importance of indirection as female methodology. Linguists tell us that women more often than men end their sentences with a question—"That's a useful perception, isn't it?" A group of Boston academics with whom I spent a year reading texts by women concluded that the key female device—symbolically, not quite literally—was the parenthesis. One can speculate that women characteristically feel less comfortable than men with direct, authoritative, categorical assertion because their social experience has made them less confident, but one can also argue that the mode of indirection and qualification allows for richer inclusiveness. Perhaps women say more by saying it quietly.

And perhaps again—*I'm* speculating, of course—feminist criticism may exert powerful effects in ways quite different from those we are used to. It may work—not always, but sometimes—through its impact on individuals rather than through public pronouncements; it may triumph by refusing to define itself. Maybe its strength will come on occasion from ending its sentences with question marks.

If so, I think it will also have to be acknowledged, once more, that in its strength lies its weakness. I looked out my office window as I was writing the sentence about question marks. On the street corner just opposite stood Jacques Derrida, talking with—talking *at*—a graduate student. The student expressed rapt deference in every muscle as he smiled and nodded and looked very interested. M. Derrida radiated confidence and authority and excitement about what he was saying. I thought: would Derrida worry in print, really worry, about the *problems* implicit in his mode of criticism? Not a chance—or if he did, his role would be to resolve the problems, not to articulate them. The question marks that end his sentences do not reflect any fundamental uncertainty or tentativeness. The critical movements generally agreed to be most powerful make categorical claims for themselves. Their grandiosity may generate opposition, often heated opposition, but it also demands respect. Almost everyone takes structuralism, and post-structuralism, seriously, although not everyone by any means accepts the critical tenets of these movements. Many people manage not to take feminist criticism seriously.

It may sound as though I'm saying that the problem is to claim more authority. I'm not. The problem, it seems to me, reflects and duplicates one experienced in personal terms by many women trying to function successfully in professional and business contexts long controlled by men. If one wants to imitate the male mode, the path is relatively straightforward—not simple, but straightforward. We can study Derrida and try to do what he does. When I started writing criticism, I used to read F. R. Leavis over and over: not because I admired his doctrine; because I admired his authority. I wanted some of that too. We can put on business suits and commit ourselves to competition and dedicate ourselves to getting ahead; it's not easy, but it's not impossible. On the other hand, many women struggle for a more complicated mode of success, a mode which will not require them to become imitation men. Instead of nerving ourselves to interrupt men as often as they interrupt us, we can seek strategies to make the men embarrassed by their own aggressiveness. We can insist on putting concerns about relationship ahead of concerns about success; we can try to define a *female* way of doing things. It's quite likely, I think, that we won't rise as far, glow as brilliantly, as our more openly aggressive sisters.

Feminist criticism, and its proponents, face versions of this dilemma. We can claim the certainties traditional to effective critical practice, and try to make our criticism sound like theirs, or we can insist on multiplicity and partialness and even tentativeness, on acknowledging the uncertainties implicit in an approach which values the personal. To air one's doubts is a luxury. Feminist critics can't afford to sound too tentative in print: they would thus become once more dismissible. But there is also loss involved in sounding too authoritative—not just the danger of being damned as shrill or strident, but the danger of losing touch with traditionally female commitments which many of us value.

The implication of all I've been saying is that feminist criticism faces a larger task than competing modes usually undertake: the task not only of enforcing new ways of seeing, but also of discovering new ways of saying. Imitating Leavis is not enough, as I soon discovered, and neither is imitating Derrida. Yet we want people to pay attention. We need a larger audience; the question is how to get it without compromising the fundamental assumption that women, as subjects for fiction and biography and autobiography and as writers of all these genres and others, have inherent and substantial interest.

There is some evidence that feminist criticism is beginning to find such an audience. Modern Language Association meetings abound in feminist programs, newly rediscovered works by women—*Herland, The Yellow Wallpaper*—attract many readers, new biographies of women keep reassessing familiar figures, women's studies courses proliferate, feminists get grants to do feminist work. The National Endowment for the Humanities has supported the development of several women's studies programs; and I personally know women scholars who have received Guggenheim, Rockefeller, and American Council of Learned Societies grants, as well as support from the NEH and the American Association of University Women, for feminist projects. Matters have changed since ten or twelve years ago, when I was the only woman on a panel awarding NEH fellowships, and only one woman applicant survived the preliminary screening. (Few women had applied in the first place.) Her project didn't sound very good to any of us. "Oh, let's give her one anyhow," a panelist urged. "It will look good to have a woman." His male colleagues concurred.

It's not so easy to patronize women scholars any more; probably no one is saying quite that sort of thing in NEH circles today. Still, feminist criticism does not get a very good press. And that brings me back where I started; the only conceivable way for it to get a good press is to be dazzlingly illuminating, too good to be ignored. Women often resent the fact, or apparent fact, that they have to accomplish more, demonstrate more, than men in order to get ahead at the same rate. If it's true of women in their lives, it's equally true of their criticism. The problem is not only to make it new, but to make it better. Those of us who try to write this sort of criticism must make ever higher demands on ourselves.

Let me offer you a case in point, a little bit of fresh feminist criticism. The value of this critical mode, as of all useful modes, is that it provides unexpected ways of seeing, as a result of the new questions it raises, the new consciousness it brings to literature. Imbued by this consciousness, I have found myself reading Jane Austen differently: we really *are* back where we started. Rereading her novels recently, I found myself thinking about the tiny stories of sexual betrayal embedded in several of the texts. Sometimes, as in *Northanger Abbey,* nothing much happens: Captain Tilney flirts with Isabella Thorpe intensely enough to cause her to break her engagement with a man presumably too good for her, since he is the heroine's brother; then the captain abandons her. Lydia, in *Pride and Prejudice,* gets to marry her paramour as she wished, averting condemnation as a social outcast. Georgianna Darcy, in the same novel, is rescued in the nick of time from a potential seducer. In *Mansfield Park,* on the other side, the consequences are very serious: Maria's life is ruined by her indiscretions, and Henry Crawford loses the woman he wanted. *Sense and Sensibility* provides the most perplexing of these stories: one with dark consequences in the background and danger in the foreground. Unlike the episodes in other novels, the sexual events in *Sense and Sensibility* have no direct effect on the major characters; their female participants are known to us only by hearsay. Many readers of the novel forget the anecdote altogether, so peripheral does it seem. What is it doing there?

One can, of course, take it simply as a cautionary tale. Colonel Brandon tells the story with avowed didactic purpose. It concerns two young women named Eliza. The first Eliza grows up as the Colonel's foster sister. He and she love one another and hope to marry; on the brink of their elopement, the young man's father intervenes and forces Eliza to marry instead, for financial reasons, Brandon's elder brother. The bereaved male lover goes abroad with his regiment; the deprived female finds herself the wife of a dissipated man with no great interest in her. Eliza, still in her teens, runs away from her husband, forming sexual connections with other men. Her husband divorces her. By her first lover she bears a daughter, the second Eliza. When the Colonel returns to England, he finds her destitute and dying. He cares for her in her final weeks and promises to take responsibility for her child, whom he subsequently places in a school and later in the care of "a very respectable woman." From this woman she runs away, in *her* teens, with the cad Willoughby, object of Marianne Dashwood's infatuation. Colonel Brandon rescues her; she subsequently gives birth to a child, sex unspecified.

Colonel Brandon tells this complicated story to Marianne's sister, Elinor, just after Willoughby has jilted Marianne for a richer woman. He says he wants to make Marianne feel less desperate by revealing that she's better off without so dangerous a man. But his way of saying so, full of hesitations, suggests that he may not know his own motives. "My object — my wish — my sole wish in desiring [you to tell the story to your sister] — I hope, I believe it is — is to be a means of giving comfort — no, I must not say comfort — not present comfort — but conviction, lasting conviction to your sister's mind."[7] The tale he tells, with its emphasis on the elder Eliza, who of course has no connection with Willoughby, does not altogether support his announced purpose.

Austen provides clues for understanding what really motivates the Colonel, and she offers hints of the quite different purpose the fable serves in her own narrative. There is reason to believe that Brandon wishes to caution Marianne not about Willoughby, but about herself. Marianne is the sister marked by excessive sensibility. What she feels, she displays; and she feels a great deal. Everyone who has encountered her in recent months knows of her love for Willoughby; many, including her mother, expect their marriage. Now everyone who sees her knows of her despair over Willoughby's faithlessness. She lacks prudence, dignity, *sense;* she values spontaneity and passion. Colonel Brandon has fallen in love with her himself, but he warns her against precisely the qualities that make her attractive — warns her, in effect, that they are dangerous possessions unless she has a man to take care of her.

According to Colonel Brandon's account, the first Eliza succumbed to temptation because of the evil of one man, her husband, and because she lacked the care and guidance of another.

"Can we wonder," Brandon inquires, "that with such a husband to provoke inconstancy, and without a friend to advise and restrain her (for my father lived only a few months after their marriage, and I was with my regiment in the East Indies), she should fall? Had I remained in England, perhaps—" (p. 150). It's all his fault: only men make things happen, and keep them from happening. The repetition of disasters from mother to daughter likewise testifies to male inadequacy. "'Such,' said Colonel Brandon after a pause, 'has been the unhappy resemblance between the fate of mother and daughter! And so imperfectly have I discharged my trust!'" (p. 153). The self-referential conclusion to his narrative suggests his surprisingly grandiose sense of personal power: even his failure attests it. Though a modest man, the Colonel partakes of the masculine nature.

If he considers that men might have averted the falls of the two young women, he also believes the women's characters partly determinant of their fates. The character of the first Eliza, significantly, resembles Marianne's: "the same warmth of heart, the same eagerness of fancy and spirits" (p. 149). "'There is a very strong resemblance between them as well in mind as person,'" Brandon asserts flatly (p. 149). Warmth of heart, eagerness of fancy in a female, in other words, imply sexuality, thus extreme vulnerability. Marianne is sexy, therefore she attracts him. She is sexy, therefore she needs him to protect her from herself and from the depredations of other men. Such is the real message of the Colonel's story.

But what is its function in Austen's narrative? How can we reconcile the Colonel's point of view with the narrator's? Brandon's account of the first Eliza conveys his compassion for her lack of a male protector. We may note also her lack of a female protector, which he does not emphasize. Orphaned young, brought up by her uncle, without a mother, she displays great tenderness toward her illegitimate daughter. "'She loved the child,'" the Colonel reports, "'and had always kept it with her'" (p. 151). The child is an "it" to the Colonel, but clearly not to the mother, for whom her daughter and namesake provides the only constant human tie. Her pseudo-sibling and avowed lover, after all, has deserted her. He has done so from noble motives, with the best intentions, but his abandonment could have been no more complete had he had evil purpose. Perhaps we can see in the tale of the two Elizas a fable of female need. The second

Eliza, too, lacks a mother from the age of three, and her guardian has consigned her first to institutional care, only much later to the respectable woman. She too may seek love to compensate for deprivation.

So interpreted, the Eliza story calls attention to important issues in the central plot. Even Austen admirers often find *Sense and Sensibility* the least memorable of her novels. It does not present the same moral perplexities as *Mansfield Park,* yet it too seems oddly disturbing. When Marianne marries depressed Colonel Brandon, a man twice her age, yielding all her fantasies for a staid version of reality, the reader may have trouble feeling this a happy ending. Elinor, the more "sensible" sister, gets the man she wanted all along, but even that conventionally satisfactory resolution feels unsatisfying. Mother-dominated Edward Ferrars, her mate, is pretty depressed himself, and remarkably passive. Both sisters have learned predictable moral lessons: Marianne, to rely less on sensibility; Elinor, to acknowledge feeling. But their rewards prove ambiguous. By comparison with Edward and the Colonel, even Henry Tilney in *Northanger Abbey,* even Edmund in *Mansfield Park,* seem exciting companions.

Sense and Sensibility in fact tells a dark story—and the large story as well as the small one centers on female need. The young women's education involves social more importantly than moral reality. Society, they learn, operates through concealments. Everyone except the most foolish characters has a secret; everyone manipulates others by alternate concealment and revelation. Sense and sensibility, thought and feeling, become social counters. Those who learn to use them properly will get what society has to offer; but to women it doesn't offer much.

The novel begins with a rather elaborate presentation of female financial need and dependency. Left in impoverished circumstances, the Dashwood sisters and their mother hope for the benevolence of the girls' half-brother, whose father has enjoined him to take care of them. That brother, however, manages to rationalize an utter lack of generosity. The women learn to make do.

That's what women *have to* learn, the novel says. The introductory tale of financial need provides one paradigm of the female condition, the Eliza story offers another. Both say the same thing: a woman must satisfy her needs with little. To do so exemplifies the way of sense, the course the Dashwood women follow in economic matters. The alternative path of sensibility, of declaring and acting upon one's emotional demands, the path followed by the two Elizas—that way leads to disaster. Properly schooled in repression and denial, a woman will get something out of life: something, but probably not much.

It sounds like a bleak message, and the novel's tone does not feel all that bleak. The willed economy of the female Dashwoods, the willed restraint which Marianne learns and Elinor practices from the beginning need not involve misery. Wit, intelligence, and good humor operate even with limited opportunity; to make the best of things can provide a cheerful mode of existence. When Marianne, "instead of falling a sacrifice to an irresistible passion, as once she had fondly flattered herself with expecting, . . . found herself, at nineteen, submitting to new attachments, entering on new duties, placed in a new home, a wife, the mistress of a family, and the patroness of a village" (p. 275)—when she finds herself so circumstanced, her submission obviously had its compensations. Yet the verb *submitting*, in this context—"submitting to new attachments"—carries somber overtones. *Sense and Sensibility* examines the varieties of female submission; among them, Eliza's is the most lurid but not necessarily the most profound.

The last time I read *Sense and Sensibility* I saw none of this. Now it seems obvious.

It seems obvious not because of any theoretical refinements of the last ten years of criticism, but because of new ways of valuing female experience. An excursion into autobiography—a narrative of how I myself became involved in feminist criticism—may clarify the point by suggesting the close link between thinking about female lives and about female texts.

In 1969–70, I had a sabbatical leave from Wellesley College and a fellowship to finish my book on Pope. In the late summer of 1969, I met at a dinner party a man who proved to be the manuscript librarian at Houghton, the Harvard rare book library. He told me the library had just acquired a late journal by Mrs. Piozzi, five volumes of manuscript. Would I, as an eighteenth-century scholar, have a look and see if something could be written about the journal?

I felt no great interest in this task. About Mrs. Piozzi I knew only that she was Dr. Johnson's friend. Like Alice James, she had always been defined by her connections. While married to Henry Thrale, she had entertained and comforted Johnson, who spent much of his time in the Thrale household. After Thrale's death, she fell in love with an Italian musician, Gabriel Piozzi, whom she married in the face of intense opposition from family and friends. Johnson, who disapproved violently, never saw or wrote to her again. Boswell described her as a busybody and a bore; there seemed no particular reason to be interested in her.

But in late September I dutifully went to have a look. The journals turned out to have been written when Mrs. Piozzi was in her seventies, after her husband's death. She intended them for the eye of her adopted son, Piozzi's nephew; they amounted to an extended self-justification, an explanation of her life. As I read them, I kept having the uncanny feeling that I was listening to the voices of my friends. Over and over before I had heard what Mrs. Piozzi said. She wrote about the problems of being an intellectual woman; no one will ever love you for what you know, she maintained. She wrote about feeling unappreciated by her children, about her fear that her life was disappearing in service to others, about her greater fear that no one would take her seriously. With no expressed consciousness that anyone else had ever felt as she did, she articulated the difficulties of a woman struggling to declare her own value in a world which systematically denied it.

I wrote about all this, about Mrs. Piozzi's efforts to define and assert her identity, about Mrs. Piozzi as a woman. The *Harvard Library Bulletin* published my long essay without a murmur, although the editor pointed out that they'd never printed anything like it before. All the rest of the year, as I worked on Pope, I kept thinking about Mrs. Piozzi and that familiar voice I had heard through her prose. I wondered if other women writers spoke in the same voice, if one listened. The next fall, I taught a course in women writers. A year later, I began writing *The Female Imagination*. I had turned into a feminist critic.

When I read those Piozzi journals, I had no conscious commitment to the cause of women, no strong political orientation of any kind. The text, it seemed, enforced its meaning on me. My experience as a woman among women sensitized me to that meaning: a man, I suspect, would not have found the same things in the manuscript. He would, of course, have discovered other meanings, useful or provocative or ingenious, but not the ones that depend on female experience. When James Clifford wrote his scholarly biography of Mrs. Piozzi, he could not avoid communicating his distaste for her as a personality. A woman, Mary Nash, is now writing a new biography: without being less scholarly, it will sound very different. The new biography will be grounded in a new way.

If I'm right about the sources of power in feminist criticism — its flexibility, its commitment, its attention to the relation of art and life — they can imply a highly individualistic critical mode, but a mode solidly grounded in experience. Lacking a universal systematic methodology, such criticism may evolve from individual sensibilities in relation to individual texts. Since it rests on a foundation of female experience, it draws on the separate experience of the females who practise it. It lacks high priestesses to prescribe forms for their disciples. It is still young, still experimental, capable of finding new directions as its practitioners formulate them. It is not a "school," and it doesn't have the kind of influence that "schools" have in our universities; it does not tend to produce epigones.

Feminist criticism depends partly on what its writers have experienced, and it helps its readers to understand their own experience. Men can practise it too, of course, and do. They bring to it the advantages and disadvantages of an external point of view: possibly less likely than women to project their own psychic histories into the text, they also have less basis for understanding the subtleties of what belongs peculiarly to females. Men and women alike may do it badly. But it is beginning to fulfill its potential for uncovering the hidden and vital. Eventually, given the careful attention it offers to women's writing and to men's, feminist criticism will enable us to think with precision about what differences, if any, divide male and female writing. I haven't mentioned that problem, partly because it seems to me important to emphasize that making such differentiations, or attempting to make them, is by no means the only or necessarily the most significant task of feminist criticism. I have come to feel that generalizations about women's writing and men's closely resemble generalizations about women and men: although they may point to some general truths — that, after all, is what

24

generalizations are supposed to do—individual texts, like individual people, when closely examined tend to elude generalization.

But one of my points is that feminist criticism need not consist in, or depend on, only generalizations. It still has many questions to ask, as well as many assertions to offer. Its demands on the practitioner are frustrating, in moments of despair they seem hopeless—but its possibilities remain exciting. I heard a paper recently by a Renaissance scholar raising the question of how the female ruler of Elizabethan England affected contemporary authors' imagining of the gender of their audience, and what difference the gender of the Elizabethan audience might make anyhow. Even apart from its quite brilliant individual insights, the paper gave me a thrill of excitement because it so palpably dealt with issues which no one would have thought of addressing twenty years ago. As long as feminist criticism can generate such thrills it retains the potential of taking an important place in the intellectual currents of our time. Its combination of openness and solid grounding gives it fundamental strength; it has only begun to demonstrate what revelations it can produce.

NOTES

1. H. W. Garrod, "Jane Austen: A Depreciation," *Discussions of Jane Austen*, ed. William Heath (Boston: D. C. Heath, 1961), p. 35.
2. Julia Prewitt Brown, *Jane Austen's Novels: Social Change and Literary Form* (Cambridge: Harvard University Press, 1979), p. 154.
3. Sandra M. Gilbert and Susan Gubar, *The Madwoman in the Attic: The Woman Writer and the Nineteenth-Century Literary Imagination* (New Haven: Yale University Press, 1979), p. 169.
4. Annette Barnes, "Female Criticism: A Prologue," *The Authority of Experience: Essays in Feminist Criticism*, ed. Arlyn Diamond and Lee R. Edwards (Amherst: University of Massachusetts Press, 1977), p. 9.
5. Mary Poovey, "My Hideous Progeny: Mary Shelley and the Feminization of Romanticism," *PMLA*, 95 (1980), 332–47.
6. Annette Kolodny, "Some Notes on Defining a 'Feminist Literary Criticism,'" *Critical Inquiry*, 2 (1975), 75–93.
7. *The Complete Novels of Jane Austen*, I (New York: Vintage, 1976), 148.

NEW DIRECTIONS FOR FEMINIST CRITICISM IN THEATRE AND THE RELATED ARTS

NANCY S. REINHARDT

I.

WOMEN'S STUDIES IN CINEMA and popular culture are thriving. The feminist perspective in film studies has inspired nearly a decade of lively dialogue and the beginnings of what will soon be a substantial tradition of feminist film criticism. Not long after the women's movement became a political reality, critics and sociologists began writing about images of women in film; comparable feminist studies of television and popular culture were not far behind. A new film journal was born and, although it lasted only a few years, it was soon replaced by sister publications.[1] Feminist conferences, colloquia, lectures are now held regularly, and the principal tenets of this young critical tradition seem so persuasive that feminists no longer feel they must restrict their scholarship to safer, traditional lists of the stereotypical images and themes of a capitalist patriarchy. They are now experimenting with some of the newer and perhaps more controversial critical fashions from Europe.

Women's studies in theatre criticism, however, is relatively new and in theatre history only just beginning. Theatre (including opera) is the most traditional and conservative member of the consortium of dramatic and related media arts. It is an ancient art, much older than prose fiction, and probably as old as ritual itself. It is an art rich in history and can trace a critical tradition at least as far back as ancient Greece. Throughout history, in responding to new aesthetic developments, play-

Nancy Reinhardt is the Director of Special Students in the Faculty of Arts and Sciences at Harvard University. She also lectures in theatre and film studies. Her research interests include modern drama, Swedish film and theatre, and the history of scene design.

wrights and other creative artists of the classical, mainstream stage have tended to lag behind the other major traditional arts. Naturalism, for example, was accepted as a valid concern of prose fiction and painting long before the average European or American theatre-goer could tolerate it on the "legitimate" stage.[2] Aware, perhaps, of this strongly conservative tradition, theatre historians and critics have been slow to react to the latest critical trends. Just as we are only beginning to see (Anglo-American) theatre scholars trying out new modes such as semiology (a critical posture that has been around for more than a decade in film studies), so are we only beginning to see them responding to the challenges of women's studies in their analyses of the traditional theatre classics.[3]

Although there may be many other explanations, I will outline three possible reasons for this apparent discrepancy between feminist film and feminist theatre criticism, why theatre scholarship has been essentially so conservative in contrast to many innovative feminist film studies.

First, film and television, compared to theatre, are young media—children of the twentieth century. The relative newness of film-and-media studies, then, has contributed to the growth and flexibility of its feminist literature. A younger discipline does not have to carry around centuries of critical baggage—the traditional debates, the academic discourse, the many definitions and postulates. It therefore tends to be more responsive to new perspectives and challenges in its search for a pertinent critical vocabulary.

Another reason for this burgeoning of feminist film-and-television criticism is the obvious sexist content of the media. Hollywood and network television, the most influential image-makers in the United States, create quite explicitly the roles and starry faces that the powerful box-office fathers and advertisement moguls believe will sell more effectively. Theatre is, of course, not exempt from the pressures of the box office, but the proprietors of the traditional stage prefer to maintain at least the illusion of respectability. In mainstream film and television, however, exploitation of women is often so explicit that few good feminists have been able to resist attacking the sexist images on all fronts. Hence the critical arsenal developed boldly and quickly.

My third point is the most speculative and yet is central to the argument of this paper. Theatre studies are conservative and slow to respond to new critical perspectives such as feminism because theatre is essentially—almost by definition—a public, social and hence a male-dominated art. It has been run by and for men throughout most of its history and has, for the most part, reflected current political and social realities, deferring to the taste of the political majority. Of all the arts, theatre and opera are probably the most public. Even the creative process of mounting a production necessitates more public group compromises than private individual decisions. Public audience response to the entire social event is an important part of the theatre experience. The way people respond to each other during the play and during the intermissions is almost as significant as the way they respond to the play itself.

Cinema is also a very public art, dominated by male authorities and created by a series of group compromises. But, unlike a theatre presentation which *demands* a live audience with verbal, social interaction among different people, a film can conceivably be created, like a painting, by one individual, and can be composed entirely of abstract, non-verbal (non-social) imagery. It does not have to be a group effort and it does not have to evoke a live audience response; audience participation tends to be relatively personal and private. Although a film is often shown in public, the finished product is fixed, constant, and does not change with audience participation. It is viewed in the privacy and dark anonymity of the cinema house. Although often present in the movie auditorium, audience reaction is not an essential ingredient to the film experience—not in the way that it is to the theatre experience. One usually goes to a film alone, or with a friend, and the presence of others seems only an awkward necessity. In this sense, seeing a film is like reading a novel in the privacy of one's home.

The same can be said of television. The small tube in a portable box was designed for family use, and the medium itself emphasizes and even exploits this domestic setting. Both television and film often use intimate close-ups and stress personal, family, and sexual themes. These are the very themes and images which are most vulnerable to the aggressive probings of a feminist critique. Therefore, in responding to the feminist perspective, media studies and some of the relatively personal literary forms such as the domestic novel are, in certain ways, far ahead of the public and social arts such as opera and the legitimate stage.

Not only is the production of a play essentially public, but also the staging conventions, the structure and content of theatre's most venerable dramatic form, tragedy, are based on the perception of public action and public settings. Historically, these staging conventions and the association of the grand, classical stage with an essentially public context remained relatively fixed until the development of romanticism and the rise of a middle-class emphasis on the private, individual and personal, domestic settings. This major shift is reflected in the nineteenth-century decline of tragedy, the wing-and-drop set, and the rise of the mixed genre and domestic box set. This development also corresponds to the nineteenth-century interest in the new "softer sciences" such as psychology and sociology. It was during this period that intellectuals and artists were beginning to see the possible complexities of human sexuality: the roots of modern feminist consciousness were planted.

Because so many excellent feminist studies and bibliographies of film and popular culture are already in print, and because a number of media conferences and periodicals manage to maintain a continuing and lively feminist dialogue, it is not necessary to supplement the already persuasive evidence of these important developments.[4] The implications of a feminist perspective and its possible impact on the future of film and popular-culture studies should be by now quite obvious. For theatre studies, however, the implications are still not so evident.

As very little has been done in the area of women's studies and traditional, classical theatre, the field is wide open for exploration. Rather than trying to analyze in more detail the limited work that has already been done, I would like to discuss two broad areas of theatre scholarship—dramatic genre and physical production—and show how a feminist perspective might be applied to them. My comments are intended to suggest possible new directions for women's studies in theatre history and criticism. I address my first remarks to the theatre critic. How might the genre of tragedy be analyzed in feminist terms? Are not the structure and domain of tragedy essentially derived from a male-dominated *public* world? I address my second remarks to the theatre historian. How might feminist thinking be applied to the standard non-verbal (pictorial) evidence that historians use to construct theories about past production? The theatre historian should re-examine this historical evidence with a lens which focuses more closely on the position of women in productions of earlier centuries. The dominant *public* action both on the stage and in the audience stresses a male world in which women are either kept to the sides, in recesses, or are placed on display for the male viewer.

II.

An entire book—a gender analysis of the very concept of dramatic content and form—could easily be written on tragedy from a feminist perspective. In a brief but important passage from their study *The Madwoman in the Attic,* Sandra M. Gilbert and Susan Gubar have suggested a possible thesis for such an analysis:

> [O]ur great paradigmatic tragedies, from *Oedipus* to *Faust,* tend to focus on a male "overreacher" whose virile will to dominate or rebel (or both) makes him simultaneously noble and vulnerable.
>
> *   *   *
>
> It is true, of course, that . . . some stories have been imagined for women, by male poets as well as male novelists. . . . [H]owever, most of these stories tend to perpetuate extreme and debilitating images of women as angels or monsters. . . . It is Macbeth, after all, who is noble; Lady Macbeth is a monster. Similarly, Oedipus is a heroic figure while Medea is merely a witch, and Lear's madness is gloriously universal while Ophelia's is just pathetic. Yet to the extent that the structure of tragedy reflects the structure of patriarchy—to the extent, that is, that tragedy must be about the "fall" of a character who is "high"—the genre of tragedy, rather than simply *employing* such stories, itself necessitates them.[5]

We should look closely at the questions that this passage raises. To what extent does "the structure of tragedy reflect the structure of patriarchy"? How does "the genre of tragedy . . . necessitate" stories about noble and glorious male "overreachers"?

Tragedy in the Western sense has, of course, been formalized by the *Poetics,* probably the most famous and influential of all documents from the history of literary criticism. Its author, Aristotle, the fourth-century Greek philosopher, scientist, and educator, was a paradigmatic spokesman for the ancient male-centered society—the city-state or *polis.* He exemplifies the ethos of one of the purest patriarchies in the history of Western society. From the time of Aquinas, through the high Renaissance, until this very day, Aristotle's influence has helped to shape the curriculum and the intellectual assumptions of the Western male-centered university. Even today a seminar in "lit crit" is not complete without at least a respectful glance at Aristotle. The *Poetics* has been considered such an authority in the description of the genre of tragedy that some instructors have even assumed that its postulates are givens. How many times have students been told that tragedy *is* "the imitation of an action that is serious and also, having magnitude, complete in itself"; and that this "imitated action" arouses in the audience "pity and fear" but then eventually results in the "catharsis of such emotions"; and that the central character serving the action is a good man (not too good) "whose misfortune is brought upon him not by vice and depravity but by some error of judgment."[6]

With this kind of authority assumed, the bemused student is then asked to take a serious classical play and try to plug it into the Aristotelian construct. If it does not fit, then it is "problematic" and perhaps not even a tragedy. *Macbeth,* then, is problematic because the tragic hero, or what Gilbert and Gubar call the "overreacher," is too dark, even evil, and does not fit the definition of a "good but not too good" character. And the play *Antigone* presents difficulties because it has not just one "overreacher" but two. One of these is a woman who talks like a man part of the time and whose fanaticism makes her seem too one-dimensional to fit the sympathetic mold of a well-rounded Aristotelian hero. *Medea* is more than problematic: some critics might not even consider it a tragedy in the most basic sense. Not only is Medea a murderer, like Macbeth, but she is also an emotional, "irrational" woman. Macbeth is more of a tragic figure because he at least overreaches in the public, political sphere. He has understandable and laudable goals. He is the medieval version of the power-hungry politician or the ambitious corporate executive who will do almost anything to attain the ultimate goal of patriarchy—being top dog in an aggressive and warlike society. Medea, however, wants to maintain her family and her rights as a woman—as wife and mother—but she is also frustrated by the limitations of her husband's society which reject her own cultural roots. Like the Furies who haunt the world of male values in *The Oresteia,* Medea represents an alien, fanatic sensibility of extreme passions, non-reason, and magical powers. She makes her exit not with a noble act of male will but with the aid of the occult, on the wings of a feminine *deus ex machina*.

The limited Aristotelian definition of a tragedy, then, encourages the student to dismiss great plays as "problematic tragedies," while a feminist perspective would perhaps emphasize these complexities and contradictions as indications of the playwrights' insight into the nature of human sexuality and sex roles. Likewise, the feminist critic would even consider inadequate an Aristotelian analysis of the "proper tragedies" which manage to fit the tightly structured Aristotelian mold.

Sophocles' *Oedipus Rex* closely approaches this Aristotelian ideal and is used as a central example in the *Poetics*. A feminist critique might see *Oedipus* as, among other things, a dramatic analysis of the complexities of sexuality and the subconscious.[7] The traditional Aristotelian perspective, however, tends to provide a reductive critique which ignores the psychological dimension of Oedipus' actions. Rather than question the ethos of a male society based on the primacy of logic, the Aristotelian critic would probably celebrate Oedipus as the paradigmatic tragic hero, the glorious sun king, the leader of men who earned his right to lead by using his superior male powers of logic to defeat the tyrannical, female-monster Sphinx. Oedipus' only flaw or "error of judgment" was his *exclusive* reliance on his own powers of reasoning, the single force of the syllogism. Aristotle would perhaps have counseled him that in order to be an effective ruler one must also be wise: "wisdom must be intuitive reason combined with scientific [practical] knowledge."[8] That is, reason must be tempered with an understanding of the world as it actually is. To control one's destiny and to maintain political order, man should always be alert to the possibility of the irrational or the unpredictable: in spite of man's superior powers of reasoning, the darker forces (female?) still exist. And they retain an unexpected power just because of their inferior irrational nature.

In the Aristotelian sense, wisdom means, among other things, knowing the nature of inferior creatures — the slaves and women of daily life who are ruled more by the private passions and coincidences of the body than by the public reasoning and planning (plotting?) of the mind. The wise man watches his inferiors and keeps them under control at home in the back room or upstairs. In her study *Goddesses, Whores, Wives, and*

Slaves: Women in Classical Antiquity, Sarah B. Pomeroy provides a vivid description of the way women of classical Greece were restricted to an unattractive and oppressive home environment:

> The separation of the sexes was spatially emphasized. While men spent most of their day in public areas such as the marketplace and the gymnasium, respectable women remained at home. In contrast to the admired public buildings, mostly frequented by men, the residential quarters of Classical Athens were dark, squalid, and unsanitary.
>
> Women stayed at home not only because their work did not allow them much chance to get out but because of the influence of public opinion.
>
> * * *
>
> The separation of the sexes was expressed in private architecture by the provision of separate quarters for men and women. Women usually inhabited the more remote rooms, away from the street and from the public areas of the house. If the house had two stories, the wife along with female slaves lived upstairs. The sexes were separated to restrain the household slaves from breeding without the master's permission.[9]

The feminist scholar would emphasize that one should be fully aware of these patriarchal prejudices before trying to analyze the plays of ancient Greece.

Aeschylus, for example, dramatized in *The Oresteia* several powerful patriarchal values and assumptions. In order for the superior male *polis* to thrive under the sign of Athena (the goddess born not of woman but from the head and mind of the male god Zeus), the Furies—representatives of the matriarchy, kinship and emotional bonding to the mother—had to be tamed as the Eumenides and kept at home by the hearth. In contrast, the citizen male thrived in the open public arena. Women are to be kept at home, away from the public domain, while men are the politicians, the heroes, the creators of the public actions. Because the Aristotelian hero, the protagonist, is the *doer* (the creator) of the manly action which defines the male public domain, he must by definition be a man (or at least man-like).

Although Aristotle does not say explicitly that a tragic character should not be a woman, he certainly implies that such a choice would at least be inappropriate. First he indicates that the hero must be good, and he explains that such "goodness is possible in every type of personage, even in a woman or a slave, though the one is perhaps inferior, and the other a wholly worthless being"

(*Poetics,* pp. 55-56). But then he argues that the character must also be appropriate. Since it is, for example, "not appropriate in a female Character to be manly, or clever" (p. 56), it is, by implication, not appropriate for a female character to be the tragic hero—the one who is the master of the dramatic action, the "manly and clever" doer. In the *Politics* Aristotle clearly states that the male is born to rule the inferior female: ". . . the male is by nature superior and the female inferior; and the one rules, and the other is ruled; this principle, of necessity, extends to all mankind" (Ross, p. 292). He describes the biological basis of this theory of the inferiority of women in *De Generatione Animalium:* ". . . the female is, as it were, a mutilated male, and the catamenia are semen, only not pure; for there is only one thing they have not in them, the principle of soul" (Ross, pp. 194–95). Although the uterus has its own secretion (catamenia), it is inferior to the semen in its role in procreation. The semen provides the germ, the very "soul" of creation, while the "catamenia" only help to nurture this male soul. If the offspring is female, it is only a mutilated male, missing the key male member. The "member" creates the semen which is the creative force and the "necessary cause" of the superior male.

Again, such an observation is not unique to Aristotle but can be traced back at least to the time of Aeschylus. In *The Oresteia* patricide is regarded as a more horrible crime than matricide because the child's father is the provider of the soul, the creative germ, while the mother is only the nurturing vessel. Apollo clearly explains this distinction:

> The mother is no parent of that which is called
> her child, but only nurse of the new-planted seed
> that grows. The parent is he who mounts. A stranger she
> preserves a stranger's seed, if no god interfere.
> (11. 658–61, trans. R. Lattimore)

Hence Orestes feels compelled to kill his mother to avenge the murder of his father, his true parent. In the patriarchy real kinship is through the father not the mother, and the old-fashioned Furies (the matriarchy) who persecute Orestes for his matricide are the losers. They are domesticated and ruled by a patriarchal concept of justice: trial by jury based on logical debate and concrete evidence instead of the primitive emotions of the matriarchy. These final trial scenes of Aeschylus' trilogy dramatize the establishment of the patriarchal courtroom as the center for rational debate.

With an understanding of this patriarchal concept of kinship, and from a feminist perspective, the traditionally "problematic" tragedy *Antigone* can perhaps be reinterpreted. The passage which is particularly troublesome to the Aristotelian critic looking for a consistent tragic hero is Antigone's penultimate speech, before she is led away to her tomb. She justifies her decision to bury her outlaw brother:

> And yet the wise will know my choice was right,
> Had I children or their father dead,
> I'd let them moulder. I should not have chosen
> in such a case to cross the state's decree.
> What is the law that lies behind these words?
> One husband gone, I might have found another,
> or a child from a new man in first child's place,
> but with my parents hid away in death,
> no brother, ever, could spring up for me.
>
> (11. 905–12, trans. E. Wyckoff)

Critics have had various difficulties with this speech (see Pomeroy, p. 101). Antigone seems to be backing off, undercutting the intensity of her commitment to the ancient kinship law which demands that the dead be buried regardless of the quality of the life actually lived. It seems, then, to render more problematic Antigone's willingness to die for what now is only a partial cause. She is willing to die for her traitorous brother but would not have made such a sacrifice for her own husband or child. Some critics have argued that this passage may be a later interpolation, while Dudley Fitts and Robert Fitzgerald have even omitted it entirely from their poetic translation. The point is, however, that given this ancient Greek theory about procreation, Antigone, as mother, would not share the soul of her child, the seed of her husband: she would only be a passive receptacle nurturing that soul. Antigone nevertheless is linked by blood ties through her own father's seed to her brother who is unique and cannot be replaced.

While Pomeroy discusses the theme of blood ties in *Antigone*, she does not explore the ideological roots of these feelings of kinship. She emphasizes instead the masculine tendencies of Antigone, who refuses to be the typical female:

The preference for the brother is also characteristic of the masculine woman, who may reject the traditional role of wife and mother as a result of being inhibited by external forces from displaying cherishing or nurturing qualities. The masculine woman often allies herself with the male member of her family.

(Pomeroy, p. 101)

Although she notes that Antigone in the end "reverts to a traditional female role," lamenting "that she dies a virgin, unwed and childless," Pomeroy argues that Antigone for the most part acts more like a man. She scorns her sister Ismene's belief that as women they should "obey the men in power" (1. 67). Antigone not only refuses to play the domestic, obeisant role of the female, but she also dares to defy publicly the law of the head of state. Referring to herself "with an adjective in the masculine gender" (Pomeroy, p. 100), she acts like a daring male hero and accepts her inevitable tragic fate. Such a description of Antigone as a kind of feminist, a masculinized woman, or an androgynous being,[10] makes her seem more consistent with the traditional Aristotelian notion of the tragic hero as masculine "doer," a bold "overreacher." The only way, it seems, for a female character in classical tragedies to emerge as a possible tragic hero is for her to be contradictory or problematic in some way—masculinized, exaggerated, or rendered abnormal like the angel or monster described by Gilbert and Gubar.

In questioning whether or not "the structure of tragedy reflects the stucture of patriarchy," one should examine not only the nature of character and the tragic hero but also the structure and moral dimension of the tragedy itself. This approach may lead one into even more controversial territory, but the results are revealing and worth the risk.

The structure of traditional Western drama, an "imitation of an action," is linear, leading through conflict and tension to a major climax and resolution. Typically, in classical theatre, the protagonist confronts the antagonist in a struggle or *agon* as intense as that suggested by the English cognates "antagonistic" and "agony." This dramatic tradition of mental and physical struggle (combat) derives from or is related to the ancient Greek practice of encouraging male citizens to compete intensely in body and mind. The concept of manly debate, the competitive use of the syllogism and the clever art of rhetoric, can be traced back well before the time of Aristotle. It was the Greeks who developed the basic definition of the university as no more, really, than a log with the teacher sitting on one end and the student at the other, struggling with each other in lively dialogue or debate. Traditional humanist drama developed from this concept and flourished throughout the centuries, particularly among the university wits of the Renaissance. Therefore when Apollo and Athena banished the old-fashioned, female ritualized activities of the Furies to the domestic hearth and established a court of law for the *polis*, they contributed to the notion of drama as considered debate rather than simply as impassioned ritual.

In describing what she calls "the masculine adversary style of discourse" (see note 11) which has prevailed in the traditionally male university with its institutionalized sex bias, Adrienne Rich quotes Walter J. Ong as one of the "few male scholars" who seem to be aware of this bias. The passage from Ong is quite striking and is worth re-quoting in full:

> Rhetoric . . . developed in the past as a major expression of the rational level of the ceremonial combat which is found among males and typically only among males at the physical level throughout the entire animal kingdom. . . . Rhetoric became particularly attached to Learned Latin, which the male psyche appropriated to itself as an extrafamiliar language when Latin ceased to be a "mother" tongue (that is, was no longer spoken in the home by one's mother). Latin, spoken and written for 1500 years with totally negligible exceptions only by males, became a ceremonial polemic which set the style for all education until romanticism. For until the romantic age, academic education was all but exclusively focused on defending a position (thesis) or attacking the position of another person—even medicine was taught this way.[11]

The history of tragedy follows nearly the same path that Ong describes for the history of rhetoric. And this is the path that takes us back at least to Aristotle, and this is the bias that legislates in the *Poetics* many of the key distinctions about tragedy. The typical dramatic structure of tragedy is based on male experience of intellectual and physical conflict, the climax and development of the emotions of pity and fear, and the catharsis of these essentially negative ("effeminate"?) emotions in the final resolution. The dramatic structure is linear and necessary; the plot can be complex but should not contain anything inconsistent or superfluous—no extra ("feminine"?) flourishes. There should be a "clear beginning, middle, and end" (*Poetics*, p. 40), and all action should lead inexorably toward that end or resolution of the conflict. One could even say that this aggressive build-up, sudden big climax, and cathartic resolution suggests specifically the typical male *sexual* response. In a letter to his friend John Murray (2 April 1817), Byron, one of several romantic poets who attempted to revive the ancient art of tragedy, noted the partiality of the genre to the male sex: "when Voltaire was asked why no woman has ever written a tolerable tragedy, 'Ah (said the Patriarch) the composition of a tragedy requires *testicles*.'"[12] So, by definition, tragedy has testicles and is written by and for those who have testicles.

Once we admit the personal world of individual feelings, contradictions, dreams, repetitions, loose associations, and the unconscious (the "ovaries"?), it is difficult to return to the world of Aristotle. The rise of mixed genres and other complexities and contradictions explored during the romantic and modern periods (along with the rise of the significance of female experience) meant the decline of tragedy in the Aristotelian sense. It would be incorrect to suggest that ancient rituals have their roots *exclusively* in a female-centered world. Nevertheless, it is interesting to note that experimentalists searching for new dramatic forms often return to ancient rituals which are associated more with matriarchy (with, for example, the female worshipers of Dionysus) than with the patriarchal (Apollonian) political sensibility. A decided male bias has dictated the tenets of classical critical taste, but a recognition of the importance of a "female perspective"—an awareness of rituals, repetitions, natural cycles, passions, family concerns—may encourage broader interpretations of the themes explored in the classics and inspire new approaches to the theatre. Rather than the linear "masculine adversary style of discourse" of classical theatre, cyclical ritual patterns, autobiographical layerings, what may be called an associative style, are perhaps more appropriate for expressing the female experience (and, indeed—as the women's liberation movement has also revealed—many aspects of the *male* experience). Nineteenth-century experimental playwrights made this discovery, and recently writers such as Megan Terry and Ntozake Shange, inspired by an invigorated movement in women's theatre, have been experimenting freely with these different forms. The feminine perspective, the reinterpretations of the classics, the "new forms," all suggest that women may indeed have their own way of seeing and feeling, and that their insights must not be ignored. A few philosophers and psychologists writing today in respectable books and journals have even proposed the startling thesis that women might in some situations *think* differently about basic moral and practical questions, and that such female experience and insights are equally valid and should no longer be suppressed.[13] Intuitively, women have known this for generations. One need only to look at the madness of NATO generals playing nuclear war games on a mock battlefield of Europe to see that a woman's perspective about combat and "heroic struggle" is sorely needed. Somehow, the traditional male assumption that there is something morally superior about the "tragic hero" who fights and kills and dies for a "great idea" (often without regard even for the quality of that idea) is just plain perverse and morally corrupt. At the very least, a feminist perspective should help the critic to reinterpret the great moral questions of the classic tragedies and to perceive the corresponding shift in modern taste in different and morally refreshing terms.

Finally, it is not just the characters, the structure, and the moral framework of traditional plays that could perhaps be interpreted differently from a feminist perspective. Our sense of the imagery and language itself probably would be radically altered. At least that is what one woman of the theatre, Mildred Janz, believes. In her essay "Ours Is a Theater of and by Man; and Now We Need a Theater of Woman," she gives an example of the way in which a woman might have rewritten a tragedy in the classical repertory:

> For instance, a woman would never have written the words of Shakespeare's *Hamlet:*
> "To be or not to be; that is the question:
> Whether 'tis nobler in the mind to suffer
> The slings and arrows of outrageous fortune . . ."
> If Hamlet (Shakespeare) were a woman, the words would have been more: Should I expose my mother, uncle and their deeds? — every act I do from now on will pivot on my decision. But if Shakespeare were a woman, he would not have given Hamlet this choice, for the answer in his mind would have been predetermined. A woman does not decide to have a baby once she is pregnant.
> Queen Gertrude asks:
> "Alas, how is't with you
> That you do bend your eye on vacancy

And with the incorporal air do hold discourse?"
This was written by a man who did not know that the inside woman
questions constantly. Gertrude should have accepted Hamlet's stare
as simple daydream. Inside women believe in daydreams, and respect the daydreams of others.[14]

Many articles, even books, have been written on gender and the
use of language.[15] The implications of such studies for feminist
analyses of language in the theatre need to be developed.

III.

Now to turn from tragedy to my second broad illustration of
the way in which women's studies could stimulate new directions
in theatre scholarship. I will look at several examples from the
history of theatrical staging and show how a gender analysis of
the visual imagery could help to describe the social context and
ideological content of the plays.

The study of visual imagery and gender has its obvious
applications to the theatre, especially in the analysis of stage
directions and physical stage imagery. Just as there seem to be
differences in the way men and women use language, so, apparently, are there differences in the way men and women create
and use visual images. In both cases these differences help to
define the power relationship between men and women. The
question whether men *naturally create* visual images that are
different from those of women is clearly controversial.[16] But it
seems obvious enough that men often *use* visual imagery
differently—especially when the imagery includes views of
women in relationship to men. In *Ways of Seeing,* John Berger
brilliantly analyzes how male artists have traditionally created
imagery and compositions which express the power of the male
patron (the owner of the paintings) over women as their prize
property.[17] He explains how historically the primary viewer of a
painting of a nude woman has been its male owner. This fact has
led to the creation of a tradition in painting of female nudes in
which the body is objectified and placed voyeuristically on
display. This tradition does not presume a female viewer.
Therefore, if a woman looks at a nude painting, the whole
tradition is called into question. The same point holds for
theatre: the tradition assumes for the most part a male audience
and tends to create sexual imagery only for men.

It would be naive to ignore the voyeuristic element of Western theatre, with those ankles and those breasts partially exposed by the most fashionably revealing dresses of the period! Even the traditional proscenium arch is shaped like a magic picture or window frame to reveal exotic and occasionally titillating sights to spark the dull senses of the jaded male. As if to flaunt the voyeuristic potential of the peep-hole proscenium-arch structure, Baroque designs for court theatres often would decorate the stage opening itself with elaborate, sexually suggestive feminine curves. In many of the extant designs, the pillars and niches exude a voluptuous atmosphere with chubby *putti* and full-breasted women partially clothed in vaguely classical gowns.[18]

Recent studies of literature, especially of prose fiction, have actively addressed the phenomenon of changing relationships between reader and text.[19] Criticism which questions the absolute authority of the work itself, and which stresses the importance of varying audience participation, is particularly useful to the feminist critic searching for new ways to describe gender relationships. Comparable studies are needed for the theatre, especially for the visual components of the stage production itself—the voyeuristic elements and the changing power relationship between men and women on the stage and in the audience. As Linda Walsh Jenkins explains in her introduction to the chapter "Images" in the recently published essay collection, *Women in American Theatre,* visual analysis in theater in general is relatively new, especially in the area of specific gender analysis:

> Theatre studies have only begun to explore the nature of image-making in performance, the relationship of theatre images to social reality, the difference between the stage image and the image embedded in the literary text.
>
> * * *
>
> As we have only begun to ask the necessary questions in our pursuit of the meaning and implication of stage images, we cannot expect to find a vast body of research and analysis of the subject. . . . But clearly a rigorous approach to the study of gender and theatre is needed and has much of value to yield to us. We need research that considers the visual image/icon on stage as it is shaped by director/performer/designer: What gender values are being reinforced or created by the "stage picture" alone? We need more study of audience response to the apparent experience of the theatre event: How closely will they allow it to approximate their perception of actual experience and how much challenge will they allow? Is there a

gender differentiation with respect to who really censors stage images that challenge socially institutionalized images?[20]

It is one thing to attend a live show or to examine recent well-documented stage performances expecting to complete a gender analysis of "image-making in performance." But it is quite another task to analyze what is only minimal visual evidence from theatre history for the "gender values" suggested by the "stage images." The pictorial evidence historians use to reconstruct theatre environments of earlier centuries is sparse and problematic. All we have are the few paintings, engravings, mosaics and sketches which in some way seem to represent stage performances from the past. A seventeenth-century engraving depicting a scene from a contemporary play is probably not an accurate and realistic representation of the actual event but instead some combination of reportage and pictorial convention. As minimal and problematic as it might be, however, this evidence is available and is continually being re-examined by scholars who speculate extensively about theatres of past centuries. Historians are always developing new theories about the physical construction of theatres; the changing relationships between audience and stage space; the costuming, placement and movement of actors within that space. As far as I know, however, there have been no gender analyses of this pictorial evidence—at least not in English. Neither, apparently, are there any thorough gender studies of stage directions or of any other *verbal* descriptions of the stage imagery embedded in the text. The entire question of voyeurism in theatre has yet to be explored in detail.

The images which depict women of past centuries both on the stage and in the audience obviously reflect the actual role and position of women in society. A "subtext" to these images exists, however, and suggests a more complex relationship of women to the male world. It is important, then, for the feminist theatre historian to re-examine this kind of visual evidence of past productions and to ask some of the same questions Jenkins raises about relatively recent productions in American theatre: How do women presented in the pictorial history of physical theatre seem to relate non-verbally to men? What is their function or position on the stage and in the audience? What do these images reveal about the social context and the ideological content of the plays being produced? In trying to answer some of these questions, I will examine elements of the blocking (staging) patterns, costuming, and audience seating.

Although there have been and probably always will be disagreements about the precise details of the actual physical space of ancient, medieval, Renaissance and many other theatres from Western (and Eastern) history, there are basic generalizations most historians can accept. Any theatre, by definition really, consists of at least three basic areas: the audience area, the open acting space, and the physical elements which help to define this acting space. The three may overlap: for example, the acting and audience areas may be only loosely defined, as in the early ritual theatre when audience members were ritual participants or actors as well as onlookers. The "physical elements defining the acting space"—the "scenic area"—may be no more than a mound backing up a circle area where ritual performers interact with members of the community. Or this "scenic area" may be as elaborate as a multi-tiered facade with niches, balconies, spectacle machinery and other scenic effects. But there usually is this basic distinction between what in medieval theatre is called the *platea*—the open, neutral acting area—and the *mansions* or scenic houses which help to define the boundaries of this area. The mansions or various niches created by the "scenic area" were often used specifically to define the inner or domestic (female) space. The open, neutral acting area represented the public world of politics and other male-dominated activities. Even the simplest street theatre would have some kind of neutral platform and surrounding street space for the main action of the plays. The platform would typically have backdrops, curtains or scaffolding which would reveal an inner niche or confined domestic space.

Traditionally, in tragedies or serious *drames,* stage-center (the open neutral acting space) is reserved for men—for the protagonists, the tragic heroes, the "doers" of the main action. The sides, background, niches and balconies function as the inner domestic space where the woman usually are kept. Similarly, in the audience, the central public orchestra area, or the space nearest to the acting area, has been traditionally reserved for men. Here the men participate in the social event, often as voyeurs or as supporters of a particular political or intellectual position. The few women in the audience are depicted historically as remaining in the background, in balconies or private boxes. If a woman enters that public male space, she must be properly escorted by a man. Otherwise, a distortion or disguise of normal sexual roles occurs. If, in the audience, she sits with the men down front near the stage, she is probably someone's mistress or whore. If, as a character on the stage, she defies convention and invades the male central stage area, she is often exaggerated or distorted as "an angel or a monster." Rarely does the proper (normal) female character of classical tragedies or of traditional serious plays take the center stage as the initiator of the public action. Only the androgynous Antigones dare question publicly the male ship of state. Most female challenges to the male will are kept within the domestic interiors—the private comic niches, wings, bedchambers and romantic gardens. If a woman is not an Antigone and yet still seems to be challenging the male will in public (either as a female character or as an actress asserting her stardom on the commercial stage) her boldness is probably only an illusion. She is probably only contributing to the inherent voyeurism of the theatre.

Medieval theatre provides vivid examples of these arrangements. More often than in any other major theatre period, theatre of the Middle Ages relies on stereotyped characters. Medieval playwrights have drawn most of their stories from the Bible or from existing allegorical or morality tales; hence their characters tend to represent good and bad qualities. The central male characters of these plays, however, tend to be more human and sympathetically rounded than the female characters. The women characters are usually kept in the peripheries as inferior or one-dimensional, passive supporters of the male action. The proper wife or maid stands or sits to the side, occupying domestic spaces, or she retires to the bedchamber or the virgin balconies. Her main function is to frame or support the stronger male characters who dominate the central stage area. If she is brought into the central male space, she is distorted or exaggerated as an obvious stereotype of the good or the bad, the angel or the monster: Mary the virgin mother, Eve the temptress, or Noah's wife the stubborn shrew.

In the fifteenth-century *Second Shepherd's Play*, the wife, Gill, remains within the confined niche area (probably partially enclosed by curtains representing the domestic interiors) giving "birth" to sheep babies, while the witty and colorful husband,

Mak, freely moves about the streets and fields—in the open acting space—participating in the "public commerce" of the shepherds' society. Then, at the end, when the comic madonna Gill becomes the holy virgin bearing the Christ child, she, as the central female figure, is still seated and enclosed in the manger frame. Mary, the mother of God, remains in a passive and neutral pose. She is framed as the passive receptacle of God's will, displayed as a symbol of the patriarchal vision of the Catholic Church: the good and holy woman representing the most profound role a woman can hope to play—the saintly, pure and infinitely patient mother and protectress of the divine (male) will.

This symbolic use of the acting space, suggested by the action of the text, is apparently corroborated by the many pictorial depictions of comparable medieval dramatic scenes.[21] The woman typically sits within a niche, on display in all her spiritual finery, or she stands to the side framing the main action. The man goes forth into the public spaces, generating the dramatic action, the conflicts and resolutions. A feminist critic would explore the social and ideological roots of these images and apparent staging practices: What are the sexual implications of a theatre which confines the female figure to private recesses or puts her on display as an object for possession, adoration, or loathing? Why does the medieval theatre tend to use more stereotypes for women than for men? What is the relationship between the patriarchal foundations of the Catholic Church and the development of liturgical drama?

The distinction between the central male space and the peripheral female space is also evident in other periods of traditional, classical theatre history.[22] The classical Greek playwrights and even Shakespeare, who developed some of the brightest and most colorful female characters in dramatic literature, reveal this dichotomy. In these plays, the woman character typically stands quietly or sits patiently in support of the stronger male characters who tend to occupy the central stage area. When she does take the center stage, she is often exaggerated or distorted as very good or very bad. As "very good," she might dominate the "serious" center-stage space as mother-virgin-angel-saint, encased in a central birth or death frame—a holy manger or sacrificial tomb. As "very bad," she might be seen hovering in a central cave concocting her wicked brew or weaving her evil wiles among the more public spheres where men rule, tempting them from the reasonable "frame of righteousness." Or, at the very least, if she moves into the conspicuous central male-space, she is depicted as abnormal or unusual in some way. As an Antigone, she speaks and acts more like a man than a woman. As a Lady Macbeth, she denies her "female softness" and becomes unnaturally hard and ambitious, eventually losing her sanity. Even Medea and Cleopatra have a bit of the witch or magic in them which colors and eventually corrupts the disciplined male realm. Ophelia is only a weak sacrificial victim; Gertrude is also a weak woman who seems ignorant of Claudius' plottings and is depicted as a woman who is searching mostly for security and sexual gratification. While Romeo and Juliet are both impulsive and full of spontaneous love, it is Juliet who remains inside on the balcony, in the bedchamber, or in the protective gardens. When she ventures outside, she is only on her way to Friar Lawrence, to get married and to die in the ultimate inner space of her tomb, the purified marriage womb of her final love-in-death scene. Romeo, however, can play around on the streets with his friends; on occasion he is called to defend heroically the family honor. Desdemona remains chastely within the domestic interiors. While she is linked to the bedchamber, Othello is associated with battleships at sea, exotic expeditions, and the defense of honor, justice and peace on the public streets.

In contrast, comedy often depicts strong women as the well-tempered "doers" of the central action. As with the novel, however, comedy has as its natural milieu the domestic realm where women are able to wield more influence. Centerstage is as likely to represent domestic interiors as public exteriors. Therefore, Congreve's brilliant Millamant can take the center stage on an equal footing with her equally brilliant male counterpart, Mirabell. But this is "the way of the world" of comedy, where women often command the domestic central stage; Congreve's world is not the domain of tragedy with its open spaces where male heroes perform public, dramatic actions. If a female character of comedy leaves the private domestic space for the public exterior, she must do so in the proper company of a man. If she goes out of her own, she probably is a fallen woman, or an ornamental courtesan up for display or sale. She may be a worldly wise, motherly woman like Mistress Quickly, who creates a home away from home for the men who need rest from the public demands of war and politics. If the clever ingénue is compelled by circumstances to leave the domestic space, she must put on the disguise of a male so that she can move freely within the male open spaces (Rosalind and Viola).

In Western theatre, the history of costume also reflects the dual function women have played in traditional theatre as inferior or passive support characters or as display objects for men's titillation or abhorrence.[23] The costuming tends to reinforce the distinctions in the staging between the central male space and the peripheral female space.

In demure support roles, a woman character would wear conservative or less showy garb to minimize her presence, as she stands to the side or in the background, in deference to the men who would often be more exotically and strikingly dressed. See the example of James Quin in the role of Coriolanus: Quin is ostentatiously dressed in the *habit à romaine* with plumed helmet and stiff, flared tunic. The women in contrast wear contemporary dress with only a few swatches of extra cloth sewn on the sleeves and the waists of their dresses.[24] Even the famous actresses who insisted on exotic dress to make them more noticeable apparently were not always as handsomely bedecked as their male counterparts. As Margot Berthold explains in her *A History of World Theatre,* the famous eighteenth-century French actress Mlle. Clairon supposedly dressed in oriental garb for Voltaire's *L'Orphelin de la Chine.* But actually she is seen in the illustrations as clothed in fashionable, contemporary crinolines.[25] In contrast, the men playing opposite her wear the more elaborate plumes and tunics.

If the actress plays more than support roles and is drawn from the peripheries into the public male space, she is often displayed in costuming which emphasizes her goodness or her badness. If on spiritual display as a kind of madonna, or at least as a virginal innocent, she probably wears a simple modest dress to emphasize her purity. If, however, she is asked to display her sexual charms, she is given a revealing bodice or her skirts are hitched up above the ankles. Even the female characters who choose to enter the central male space on their own as initiators of the public action usually wear costumes which suggest some kind of sexual distortion. The famous "breeches roles" of the English Restoration and eighteenth century illustrate this point. Relatively "liberated" actresses such as Peg Woffington sometimes played male roles for women. Although they seem to be entering the central public space as equals to the men, they are in reality contributing to the voyeuristic element of the theatre. The breeches roles were particularly titillating to a male audience interested in role-playing and sexual ambiguities: the men's breeches and tight stockings made the women look like attractive boys while at the same time revealed their shapely female legs.

Finally, the pictorial evidence of audiences from theatre history tends to support this same distinction between central male and peripheral female space in the placement of the sexes within the audience. Until the nineteenth and twentieth centuries, respectable women were expected to shun the public theatres. Special courtly productions or private occasions might make the presence of women in the audience a social necessity, but, for the most part, the public theatre world was intended as a male world—politically, socially, sexually. The mostly male audience crowded into the orchestra area close to the stage or even sat on the stage itself for the best view. They kept their wives and daughters at home, or at least had them properly vizarded and sequestered in boxes and balconies, away from leering male eyes. The few women who lingered with the men close to the performers were probably prostitutes or other women of questionable reputation. Only during the intervals, or before and after the performances, could the woman properly go "on display" as a proud ornament of society, closely escorted by her husband.

A feminist critique of the visual representations of audiences from past centuries would help to explore some of these important social and ideological distinctions. For example, David Jee's famous 1825 engraving of a medieval English pageant production is often used as a model for the possible construction of the pageant wagon.[26] A feminist would perhaps be more interested in the rather stiff medieval audience than in the actual staging. The Jee engraving probably says more in general about Victorian attitudes toward theatre audiences and sex roles than it does about the actual construction of a pageant wagon. Very few women seem to be among Jee's medieval audience and those who are either stand to the side, in the background, or peek out from the surrounding buildings. The one relatively prominent near the wagon is a family woman with one hand on her husband's arm and the other holding her child.

Not only the coarse, ribald or risqué theatre houses but also the intellectual or political theatre arenas were considered unsuitable places for the proper society woman. One of the great intellectual debates of theatre history took place in France between the classicists and the romantics during the premier of Hugo's *Hernani*. A famous pictorial representation of that debate reveals a mostly male audience.[27] The men are crowded into the central orchestra space and are sparring vigorously with each other. In the background, only a few women are visible, sitting passively in the balconies, watching the men exchange insults and bravos. If a courtesan or prostitute had decided to enter that male space, it would be evident that she was there only to sell her wares, not to participate in the critical exchange.

IV.

Men have tended to colonize stage and audience space just as they have tended to colonize the genre of tragedy. One could also say that they have colonized theatre criticism and theatre history. Theatre has been traditionally a male public world. It is not surprising, then, that the scholarship associated with this art also tends to maintain a definite male bias. The feminist critic has made a few inroads into this territory, but many broad areas are yet unexplored.

NOTES

1. *Women and Film* survived for a few years in the early 1970s. In the mid-1970s *Camera Obscura: A Journal of Feminism and Film Theory* began publishing. The most lively resources for new feminist film criticism, however, are journals which are not exclusively devoted to women and film but which are receptive to this perspective and frequently publish feminist film articles. A few notable examples include general film journals such as *Jump Cut, Film Reader, Screen, Millennium Film Journal* and feminist journals such as *Chrysalis, Quest, Heresies, Feminist Studies,* and *Women's Studies: An Interdisciplinary Journal.*
2. Although mainstream theatre has traditionally been slower than the other arts in reacting to critical trends, underground independent theatre has always been a lively testing ground for new techniques and an active forum for social protest. It was the independent theatre movement in Europe which experimented with naturalism many years before it was accepted by the public theatres. Private avant-garde theatre groups enjoy smaller audiences and do not have to please broader public taste. Hence independent theatres are the first to rebel against the basic conservatism of the theatre and to develop political theatre in response to the current political climate. Just as new Black theatre groups responded immediately to the

Black Liberation movement of the sixties, so have hundreds of regional and underground feminist theatre groups sprung up throughout the country in support of the Women's Liberation movement of the seventies. Women playwrights and theatre artists for the independent feminist theatres have worked at the frontiers of the movement along with their sisters in filmmaking.

3. The first scholarly critical responses to the challenge of women's studies in theatre were from those who described and anthologized examples of the frontiers of the feminist-theatre movement: e.g., *The New Women's Theatre,* ed. Honor Moore (New York: Vintage, 1977). The next step was for scholars to add a feminist slant to some recent biographical and sociological studies of women of the theatre, especially those caught in the star system. An intriguing recent biography which falls into this category is Angeline Goreau's *Reconstructing Aphra: A Social Biography of Aphra Behn* (New York: Dial, 1980). Quite recently critics have begun applying a feminist perspective to great playwrights such as Shakespeare: e.g., Marilyn French, *Shakespeare's Division of Experience* (New York: Summit, 1981); Coppelia Kahn, *Man's Estate: Masculine Identity in Shakespeare* (Berkeley: University of California Press, 1981). But these are, for the most part, thematic and character analyses, following the tradition of English literary criticism in which the text is primary. These studies are not unlike early examples of feminist film criticism.

4. I have already mentioned a few useful journals (note 1). There are several others which explore media as well as film topics: e.g., *Women's Studies International Quarterly* and *Journal of Popular Culture.* Many of these journals regularly include bibliographies. Even the more general feminist literary journals such as *Women and Literature* include bibliographical references to film and popular culture studies. Another useful resource is *Women in Media: A Documentary Source Book,* eds. Maurine Beasley and Sheila Gibbons (Washington, D.C.: Women's Institute for Freedom of the Press, 1977). See also bibliographies published in book-length studies such as *Hearth and Home: Images of Women in the Mass Media,* eds. Gaye Tuchman *et al.* (New York: Oxford University Press, 1978).

5. *The Madwoman in the Attic: The Woman Writer and the Nineteenth-Century Literary Imagination* (New Haven: Yale University Press, 1979), pp. 67–68.

6. *Aristotle on the Art of Poetry,* trans. Ingram Bywater (Oxford: Oxford University Press, 1954), pp. 35, 50. Quotations from the *Poetics* follow this edition.

7. Feminists interested in doing a psychoanalytical study of Sophocles' plays should begin by consulting the seminal feminist work of Juliet Mitchell: *Psychoanalysis and Feminism* (New York: Vintage, 1975).

8. *Aristotle: Selections,* from the Oxford Translation, ed. W.D. Ross (New York: Charles Scribner's Sons, 1938), p. 261. All quotations from Aristotle, other than the *Poetics,* are from this edition.

9. (New York: Schocken, 1975), pp. 79–80. One of Pomeroy's original sources for these observations is Aristotle's *Politics.* For a feminist study of the political nature and roles of women, see Susan Moller Okin, *Women in Western Political Thought* (Princeton: Princeton University Press, 1979).

10. See Carolyn Heilbrun, *Towards a Recognition of Androgyny* (New York: Harper Colophon, 1973), pp. 1–16.

11. Adrienne Rich, *On Lies, Secrets, and Silences: Selected Prose 1966-1978* (New York: Norton, 1979), p. 128. See also p. 138.

12. *Oxford Dictionary of Quotations* (Oxford: Oxford University Press, 1979), p.

50

561. I am grateful to Terry Castle for bringing this quotation to my attention.

13. For example, Carol Gilligan of the Harvard University School of Education is to publish with Harvard University Press, fall 1982, a study, with the preliminary title *In a Different Voice: Essays on Psychological Theory and Women's Development*, which suggests that women learn to think and evaluate moral issues differently from most men.

14. *Playwrights, Lyricists, Composers on Theatre*, ed. Otis L. Guernsey, Jr. (New York: Dodd, Mead & Co., 1974), p. 302.

15. See, for example, Robin Lakoff, *Language and Woman's Place* (New York: Harper & Row, 1975); Mary Ritchie Key, *Male/Female Language* (Metuchen, N.J.: Scarecrow Press, 1975); *Language and Sex: Difference and Dominance*, eds. Barrie Thorne and Nancy Henley (Rowley, Mass.: Newbury House, 1975); *Women and Language in Literature and Society*, eds. Sally McConnell-Ginet *et al.* (New York: Praeger, 1980).

16. Two pertinent studies include: Lucy R. Lippard, *From the Center: Feminist Essays on Women's Art* (New York: E.P. Dutton, 1976), pp. 80–89 and *passim;* Joan Semmel and April Kingsley, "Sexual Imagery in Women's Art," *Women's Art Journal* 1, no. 1 (Spring/Summer, 1980), pp. 1–6.

17. London: British Broadcasting Corporation and Penguin, 1972.

18. See, for example, F. Ricci's design for a Spanish Court Theatre, c. 1680, reproduced in Phyllis Hartnoll, *The Concise History of Theatre* (New York: Harry N. Abrams, 1968), p. 96 (pl. 94).

19. Recent examples include Stanley Fish, *Is There a Text in This Class?* (Cambridge, Mass.: Harvard University Press, 1980) and Harold Bloom, Paul de Man, Jacques Derrida, Geoffrey H. Hartman and J. Hillis Miller in *Deconstruction and Criticism* (New York: Continuum, 1979).

20. Eds. Helen Krich Chinoy and Linda Walsh Jenkins (New York: Crown, 1981), pp. 236–37.

21. See, for example, the miniatures from the *Mystère de la Passion* of Valenciennes, Paris, reproduced in Cesare Molinari, *Theatre Through the Ages*, trans. Colin Hamer (London: Cassell, 1975), pp. 96–101.

22. This publication, unfortunately, is unable to reproduce illustrations. The reader is invited, however, to consult the many illustrated theatre histories such as: Oscar Brockett, *History of Theatre* (Boston: Allyn and Bacon, 1969); Margot Berthold, *A History of World Theatre* (New York: Frederick Ungar, 1972). Phyllis Hartnoll's *Concise History* (note 18), Cesare Molinari's *Theatre Through the Ages* (note 21), and Jacques Burdick's *Theater* (New York: Newsweek, 1974) are also richly illustrated. Not all illustrations, of course, support this distinction in the use of space, but a significant number of them seem to do so—enough, at least, to justify my speculations. In addition to those illustrations already cited, I suggest the following examples for examination. For the "proper woman" see: the 1738 engraving by N. Dupuis of a scene from Destouches' *Le Glorieux* at the Comédie Française (Berthold, p. 484); a scene from Whitehead's *The Roman Father* with David Garrick (Brockett, p. 280); the engraving based on Watteau of a Comédie Française production (Brockett, p. 317). For the women of "questionable reputation" see: J.F. Clemens' engraving of a scene from *Jeppe of the Hill*, after a painting by C. W. Eckersburg (Berthold, p. 499); various representations of *commedia dell' arte* women, such as the wife of Pantalone in "Pantalone cornuto," Béziers: Musée du Vieux Biterrois (Molinari, p. 162).

23. A brilliant study of the changing images of men and women in fashion by

Anne Hollander provides a useful resource for the feminist analyzing the history of theatre costume: *Seeing Through Clothes* (New York: Viking, 1975).

24. Hartnoll, p. 130.
25. Berthold, p. 482. See also Molinari, pp. 193–95.
26. Berthold, p. 294.
27. Burdick, p. 115.

THE FEMINIST CRITIQUE IN
RELIGIOUS STUDIES

ROSEMARY RADFORD RUETHER

I. Sociological and Historical Context for Women's Studies in Religion

WHY WOMEN'S STUDIES in religion? To answer this question one must first survey the historical and sociological reality of women's participation in religion. One must start with the fact of women's historic exclusion from religious leadership roles in Judaism and Christianity and their consequent exclusion from advanced and professional theological education preparatory for the roles of clergy and teacher in these traditions. One could document similar histories in other world religions, such as Islam, but in this discussion we will speak primarily of Judaism and Christianity.

Many examples of this exclusion of women from leadership, teaching and education can be cited. One thinks of the dicta in Rabbinic Judaism, "cursed be the man who teaches his daughter Torah," or the comparable statement in the New Testament, "I do not permit a woman to teach or to have authority over men. She is to keep silence" (I. Tim. 2, 12). Historically women were excluded from the study of Torah and Talmud that led to the rabbinate and which, as devotion, was considered the highest calling of the Jew. In Christianity the calling of the celibate woman diverged somewhat from the traditional view of women's limitations. But the education of women in monasteries was generally inferior to that of men and usually lacked the component of secular and classical learning which was regarded as inappropriate for women. When the educational center of Christendom shifted from the monastery to the university in the

Rosemary Radford Ruether is the Georgia Harkness Professor of Theology at Garrett-Evangelical Theological Seminary. Her teaching and writing focus particularly on feminist and liberation theologies. Among her books is *New Woman/New Earth: Sexist Ideologies and Human Liberation*, Seabury Press, 1975.

twelfth century, women were generally excluded. The northern European university particularly was a male, clerical institution. The seminary is a later institution that developed after the Reformation, when universities began to be seen as too secular to provide proper theological formation for priests and ministers. Generally they have been slow to open up to women. Oberlin was the first. Its theological school allowed a few women to attend in the 1840s, but at first they were not permitted to speak in class. Methodist and Congregational seminaries had a few women by the late nineteenth century. But prestigious seminaries like the Harvard Divinity School did not open its doors to women until the 1950s. Jewish and Catholic women began entering their seminaries even later.

II. Effects of Women's Exclusion on Theological Culture

The exclusion of women from leadership and theological education results in the elimination of women as shapers of the official theological culture. Women are confined to passive and secondary roles. Their experience is not incorporated into the official culture. Those who do manage to develop as religious thinkers are forgotten or have their stories told through male-defined standards of what women can be. In addition, the public theological culture is defined by men, not only in the absence of, but against women. Theology not only assumed male standards of normative humanity, but is filled with an ideological bias that defines women as secondary and inferior members of the human species.

Many examples of this overt bias against women in the theological tradition can be cited. There is the famous definition of woman by Thomas Aquinas as a "misbegotten male." Aquinas takes this definition of women from Aristotle's biology, which identifies the male sperm with the genetic form of the embryo. Women are regarded as contributing only the matter or "blood" that fleshes out the form of the embryo. Hence, the very existence of women must be explained as a biological accident that comes about through a deformation of the male seed by the female "matter," producing a defective human or woman who is defined as lacking normative human standing.

Women are regarded as deficient physically, lacking full moral self-control and capacity for rational activity. Because of this defective nature women cannot represent normative humanity. Only the male can exercise headship or leadership in society. Aquinas also deduces from this that the maleness of Christ is not merely a historical accident, but a necessity. In order to represent humanity Christ must be incarnated into normative humanity, the male. Only the male, in turn, can represent Christ in the priesthood.

This Thomistic view of women is still reflected in Roman Catholic canon law where it is decreed that women are "unfit matter" for ordination. If one were to ordain a woman it, quite literally, would not "take," any more than if one were to ordain a monkey or an ox. Some recent Episcopalian conservatives who declared that ordaining a woman is like ordaining a donkey are fully within this medieval scholastic tradition. Whether defined as inferior or simply as "different," theological and anthropological justifications of women's exclusion from religious learning and leadership can be found in every period of Jewish and Christian thought. Sometimes this exclusion of women is regarded as a matter of divine law, as in Old Testament legislation. Christian theologians tend to regard it as a reflection of "natural law," or the "order of nature," which, ultimately, also is a reflection of divine intent. Secondly, women's exclusion is regarded as an expression of woman's greater proneness to sin or corruption. Thus, as in the teaching of I Timothy, women are seen as "second in creation but first in sin" (I Timothy 2, 13-14).

The male bias of Jewish and Christian theology not only affects the teaching about woman's person, nature and role, but also generates a symbolic universe based on the patriarchal hierarchy of male over female. The subordination of woman to man is replicated in the symbolic universe in the imagery of divine-human relations. God is imaged as a great patriarch over against the earth or Creation, imaged in female terms. Likewise Christ is related to the Church as bridegroom to bride. Divine-human relations in the macrocosm are also reflected in the microcosm of the human being. Mind over body, reason over the passions, are also seen as images of the hierarchy of the "masculine" over the "feminine." Thus everywhere the Christian and Jew are surrounded by religious symbols that ratify male domination and female subordination as the normative way of understanding the world and God. This ratification of male domination runs through every period of the tradition, from Old to New Testament, Talmud, Church Fathers and canon Law,

Reformation Enlightenment and modern theology. It is not a marginal, but an integral part of what has been received as mainstream, normative traditions.

III. The Task of Feminism in Religious Studies

The task of women's studies in religious education is thus defined by this historical reality of female exclusion and male ideological bias in the tradition. The first task of feminist critique takes the form of documenting the fact of this male ideological bias itself and tracing its sociological roots. One thinks of works such as Mary Daly's first book, *The Church and the Second Sex* (Harper, 1968), or the book I edited, *Religion and Sexism: Images of Women in the Jewish and Christian Traditions* (Simon and Schuster, 1974). These works trace male bias against women from the Scriptures, Talmud and Church Fathers through medieval, Reformation and modern theologians. They intend to show that this bias is not marginal or accidental. It is not an expression of idiosyncratic, personal views of a few writers, but runs through the whole tradition and shapes in conscious and unconscious ways the symbolic universe of Jewish and Christian theology.

The second agenda of feminist studies in religion aims at the discovery of an alternative history and tradition that supports the inclusion and personhood of women. At the present time, there are two very distinct types of alternative traditions that are being pursued by religious feminists. Within the Jewish and Christian theological academies the alternative tradition is being sought within Judaism and Christianity. However, many feminists have come to believe that no adequate alternative can be found within these religions. They wish to search for alternatives outside and against Judaism and Christianity. Some of these feminists are academically trained religious scholars who teach in religious studies or women's studies in colleges and universities and others are more self-trained writers that relate to the popular feminist spirituality movement, such as Starhawk (*The Spiral Dance*, Harper, 1979) and Z. Budapest (*The Holy Book of Women's Mysteries*, Susan B. Anthony Coven No. I, 1979).

This latter group draw their sources from anthropology and historical scholarship of matriarchal societies and ancient religions centered in the worship of the Mother Goddess rather than the patriarchal God of Semitic religions. They see the worship of the Mother Goddess as a woman's religion stemming from pre-patriarchal or matriarchal societies. This religion is believed to have been suppressed by militant patriarchal religions, but survived underground in secret, women-centered, nature religions persecuted by the dominant male religion. Medieval witchcraft is believed to have been such a female religion. Modern feminist witchcraft or "Wicca" sees itself as the heir to this persecuted goddess religion.

Writers of this emergent goddess religion draw from an anthropological scholarship of matriarchal origins that developed in the nineteenth century and which many scholars today regard as outdated and historically dubious. There has not yet been an opportunity for an adequate dialogue between these counter-cultural religious feminists and academic feminist scholarship. This is doubly difficult since goddess religion is not simply a matter of correct or incorrect scholarship, but of a rival faith stance. Most goddess religionists would feel that even if an adequate historical precedent for their faith cannot be found in the past, it should be created and they are creating it now.

The question of the relation of Jewish and Christian to post-Christian feminist religion will be discussed again later in this paper. For the moment, I will discuss some aspects of the search for an alternative tradition within Judaism and Christianity and its incorporation into theological education in seminaries and religious studies departments.

There now exists a fair body of well-documented studies in alternative traditions within Scripture and Jewish and Christian history. These studies show that male exclusion of women from leadership roles and theological reflection is not the whole story. There is much ambiguity and plurality in the traditions about women and the roles women have actually managed to play. For example, evidence is growing that women in first-century Judaism were not uniformly excluded from study in the synagogues. The rabbinic dicta against teaching women Torah thus begins to appear, not as a consensus of that period, but as one side of an argument—that eventually won—against the beginnings of inclusion of women in discipleship.

Similarly the teachings of I Timothy about women keeping silence appear, not as the uniform position of the New Testament Church, but as a second generation reaction against widespread participation of women in leadership, teaching and ministering in first-generation Christianity. Indeed the very fact that such vehement commandments against women learning and teachings were found in the traditions should have been a clue to the existence of widespread practices to the contrary. Otherwise, the statements would have been unnecessary. But because the documents were used as Scripture or normative tradition, rather than historical documents, this was not realized.

The participation of women in early Christianity was not simply an accident of sociology, but a conscious expression of an alternative anthropology and soteriology. The equality of men and women in the image of God was seen as restored in Christ. The gifts of the prophetic spirit, poured out again at the Messianic coming, were understood, in fulfillment of the Messianic prediction of the prophet Joel, to have been given to the "maidservants" as well as the "menservants" of the Lord (Acts 2, 17-21). Baptism overcomes the sinful divisions among people and makes us one in the Christ: Jew and Greek, male and female, slave and free (Galatians 3, 28). Thus, the inclusion of women expressed an alternative theology in direct confrontation with the theology of patriarchal subordination of women. The New Testament now must be read, not as a consensus about women's place, but rather as a conflict and struggle over two alternative understandings of the gospel that suggested different views of male and female.

This alternative theology of equality, of women as equal in the image of God, as restored to equality in Christ and as commissioned to preach and minister by the Spirit, did not just disappear with the reassertion of patriarchal norms in I Timothy. It can be traced as surfacing again and again in different periods of Christian history. The strong role played by women in ascetic and monastic life in late antiquity and the early Middle Ages reflects a definite appropriation by women of a theology of equality in Christ that was understood as being applicable particularly to the monastic life. Celibacy was seen as abolishing sex-role differences and restoring men and women to their original equivalence in the image of God. As the male Church deserted this theology, female monastics continued to cling to it and understood their own vocation out of this theology. The history of female monasticism in the late Middle Ages and the Counter-Reformation is one of a gradual success of the male Church in suppressing this latent feminism of women's communities. It is perhaps then not accidental that women in renewed female religious orders in Roman Catholicism today have become militant feminists, to the consternation of the male hierarchy.

Left-wing Puritanism in the English Civil War again becomes a period when the latent egalitarianism of Christian theology surfaces to vindicate women's right to personal inspiration, community power and public teaching. The reclericalization of the Puritan congregation can be seen as a defeat for this renewed feminism of the Reformation. The Quakers were the one Civil War sect that retained the vision of women's equality and carried it down into the beginnings of nineteenth-century feminism.

Finally, the nineteenth century becomes a veritable hotbed of new types of female participation in religion, ranging from the evangelical holiness preacher, Phoebe Palmer, to Mother Ann Lee, understood by her followers as the female Messiah. New theologies that attempt to vindicate androgyny in humanity and God express a sense of the inadequacy of the masculinist tradition of symbolization. Works such as *Women of Spirit: Female Leadership in the Jewish and Christian Traditions*, Rosemary Ruether and Eleanor McLaughlin (Simon and Schuster, 1979), and *Women In American Religion*, Janet Wilson James (University of Pennsylvania, 1980), or the documentary history, *Women and Religion: the Nineteenth Century*, Rosemary Keller and Rosemary Ruether (Harper and Row, 1981), trace different periods of women's recovered history in religion.

Feminists who are engaged in recovering alternative histories for women in religion recognize that they are not just supplementing the present male tradition. They are, implicitly, attempting to construct a new norm for the interpretation of the tradition. The male justification of women's subordination in Scripture and tradition is no longer regarded as normative for the gospel. Rather, it is judged as a failure to apply the authentic norms of equality in creation and redemption authentically. This is judged as a failure, in much the same way as the political corruption of the Church, the persecution of Jews, heretics or witches, or the acceptance of slavery has been judged as a failure. This does not mean that this "bad" history is suppressed or forgotten. This also would be an ideological history that tries to "save" the moral and doctrinal reputation of the Church by forgetting what we no longer like. We need to remember this history, but as examples of our fallibility, not as norms of truth.

The equality of women, as one of the touchstones for understanding our faithfulness to the vision, is now set forth as one of the norms for criticizing the tradition and discovering its best expressions. This will create a radical reappraisal of Jewish or Christian traditions, since much that has been regarded as marginal, and even heretical, must now be seen as efforts to hold on to an authentic tradition of women's equality. Much of the tradition which has been regarded as "mainstream" must be seen as deficient in this regard. We underestimate the radical intent of women's studies in religion if we do not recognize that it aims at nothing less than this kind of radical reconstruction of the normative tradition.

IV. Translation of Women's Studies in Religion into Educational Praxis

Obviously women cannot affect an educational system until they first secure their own access to it. It has taken approximately one hundred and twenty-five years for most schools of theological education to open their doors to women and then to include women in sufficient numbers for their concerns to begin to be recognized. Women began to enter theological schools of the Congregational tradition beginning with Oberlin in the 1840s and Methodist institutions in the 1870s. Only in the 1970s have some Roman Catholic and Jewish seminaries been open to women. Moreover, even liberal Protestant institutions did not experience any "critical mass" of female students until the 1970s.

Usually, access to theological education precedes winning the right to ordination. Winning the educational credentials for ordination then becomes a powerful wedge to winning the right of ordination itself. It is for that reason that there may be efforts to close Roman Catholic seminaries, at least those directly related to Rome, to women. Rumor has it (as of this writing) that a decree has been written but not yet promulgated in Rome forbidding women to attend pontifical seminaries (which would include all Jesuit seminaries, but not most diocesan and order seminaries). Women's tenure in professional schools of theology cannot be regarded as secure until they win the right to ordination. Only then can they develop a larger number of women students and attain the moral and organizational clout to begin to make demands for changes in the context of the curriculum.

Generally, demands for feminist studies begin with the organization of a caucus of women theological students. They then begin to demand women's studies in the curriculum and women faculty who can teach such courses. In many seminaries, particularly in U.S. liberal Protestant institutions, there has been some response to these demands: some women faculty have been hired, and some women's studies incorporated into the curriculum. It is at this point that we can recognize several stages of resistance to the implied challenge to the tradition.

One standard strategy of male faculty is to seek and retain one or two women on the faculty, but to give preference to women who are "traditional scholars," not feminists. This is fairly easy to do by the established rules of the guild, while, at the same time, appearing to be "objective." Feminist studies are non-traditional. They force one to use non-traditional methods and sources and to be something of a generalist. Their content is still in flux and experimentation. Rare is the person who can fulfill the expectations of both traditional scholarship and feminist scholarship equally well. So it is easy to attack such persons as "unscholarly," and to fail to tenure them in preference to those women who prefer to be "one of the boys." As of this writing there is an alarming erosion of feminist faculty talent in theological education through precisely this method. This has forced feminist scholars in theological education to band together in a new national organization, Feminist Theology and Ministry, in order to defend the employment of feminists in existing institutions of theological education.

Efforts are also underway to create new, alternative settings for women's studies in religion. For example, groups in the Boston-Washington corridor and in Chicago (largely, but not exclusively, Roman Catholic) are seriously considering the development of autonomous feminist theology schools for women, since the existing (especially Roman Catholic) institutions have proved so unfavorable to their interests.

In some other settings a decade-long struggle for women's studies in religion is beginning to bear fruit. For example, at the Harvard Divinity School, bastion of "traditional" education, a pilot program of graduate assistants in women's studies in various fields has continued for some eight years, for much of this time under constant threat of liquidation. However, a study of the program located one of its chief flaws in the lack of prestige and respect given to the women's studies teachers by the tenured faculty. As a result, a new level of funding has been developed to allow this program to be continued and eventually to be converted into a permanent research center for women in religion, with five full-time junior and senior faculty appointments. It remains to be seen whether this expanded "prestige" will not result in some of the same pressure to prefer traditional over feminist scholars.

In the development of feminist studies in the curriculum, most institutions move through several stages. The first stage is a grudging allowance of a generalist course on women's studies in religion that is taught outside the structure of the curriculum and usually by a person marginal to the faculty. The male faculty tend to feel little respect for the content of the course (about which they generally know nothing) or its instructor, and no commitment to its continuance as a regular part of the curriculum.

The second stage is when faculty begin to acquire women in one or more regular fields who are both respected as scholars and prepared to do women's studies. Women's studies courses can then be initiated that are located in the various regular disciplines of the curriculum, such as Biblical studies, Church history, theology, ethics, pastoral psychology, preaching and liturgy or Church administration. These courses, however, are taught as occasional electives. They attract only feminist students, mostly females and a few males. The rest of the student body is not influenced by them. Most of the faculty ignore them. The new material in them does not affect the foundational curriculum. In other words, women's studies in religion goes on as a marginal and duplicate curriculum. There is now a course in "systematic theology" and a second one on "feminist" theology. The foundational courses continue as before. Therefore, implicitly, they claim the patriarchal bias in theology as the "real" or "true" theology.

The third stage would come when feminist studies begin to affect the foundational curriculum itself. Here we might detect two more stages. The third stage would be when foundational curricula continue as usual, except for an occasional "ladies' day" when women's concerns are discussed. Thus, for example, one would teach twelve weeks of traditional male Church history, and then one week in which "great women" are considered. The fourth and optimum situation would be reached when feminist critique really penetrates the whole foundational curriculum and transforms the way in which all the topics are considered. Thus, it becomes impossible to deal with any topic of theological studies without being aware of sexist and nonsexist options in the tradition and bringing that out as an integral part of one's hermeneutic. Thus, for example, one would understand St. Paul as a man whose theology is caught up in ambivalent struggle between various alternatives: between an exclusivist and a universal faith, between an historical and an eschatological faith, and between a patriarchal and an integrative faith. The way he handled the third ambiguity, moreover, conditioned fundamentally the way he handled the first two ambiguities. Thus, one cannot understand Paul as a whole without incorporating the question of sexism into the context of his theology.

Generally we can say that most seminaries who have dealt with women's studies at all are somewhere between stage one and stage two, usually at stage one. A few have done an occasional "ladies' day" in the foundational curriculum. Few have even begun to imagine what it would mean to reach the optimum incorporation of feminism into the foundational curriculum, as a normal and normative part of the interpretive context of the whole. Moreover women's studies in religion has not yet matured to the point where it is able to offer a comprehensive reconstruction of methodology and tradition in various fields. For example, a genuine feminist reconstruction of systematic theology is yet to be written.

Even further down the road is the "retraining" of male faculty who are able to take such work into account. There are exceptions. Occasionally one finds that prodigy, a male professor who early recognized the value of the feminist critique and has been able, easily and gracefully, to incorporate it into his teaching with a minimum of defensiveness or breast-beating. In general, however, one would have to say that women's studies in theological education is still marginal and vulnerable. The conservative drift of the seminaries means that increasing numbers of women students themselves are non- or anti-feminist. Cadres of explicitly hostile white male students are emerging. Constant struggle is necessary to maintain momentum or even to prevent slipback. The recent publication of the book *Your Daughters Shall Prophecy* (Pilgrim Press, 1980), reflects on this ten-year struggle for feminist theological education in several major educational settings.

V. Alternative Views of Feminism and Religious Studies

Finally, we must say that feminists in religion are by no means united in what they understand to be the optimum feminist reconstruction of religion. We also have to reckon with the fact that religion is not simply an academic discipline. It is an integral part of popular culture. Concern with it has to do with *modus vivendi* of large numbers of people in many walks of life. It shapes mass institutions, the Church and the Synagogue, as well as alternative religious communities that emerge to fill people's need for life symbols. Thus, the interest in feminism and religion has an urgency, as well as a rancor, that is different from that in academic disciplines.

There are several different lines that are emerging both in academics and across the religious institutions and movements of popular culture today. One group, who could be identified as evangelical feminists, believe that the message of Scripture is fundamentally egalitarian. Scripture, especially the New Testament, proposes a new ideal of "mutual submission" of men and women to each other. This has been misread as the subjugation of women by the theological tradition. These feminists would hope to clean up the sexism of Scripture by better exegesis. It would be incorrect to interpret these evangelical feminists as always limited by a pre-critical method of scriptural interpretation. Their limitations are often more pastoral than personal. They are concerned to address a certain constituency, the members of the evangelical churches from which they come, with the legitimacy of an egalitarian understanding of Biblical faith. They sometimes limit themselves to this kind of exegesis because they know it is the only way to reach that constituency.

A second view, which I would call the "liberationist" position, takes a more critical view of Scripture. People with this view believe there is a conflict between the prophetic, iconoclastic message of the prophetic tradition, with its attack on oppressive and self-serving religion, and the failure to apply this message to subjugated minorities in the patriarchal family, especially the women and slaves. The vision of redemption of the Biblical tradition transcends the inadequacies of past consciousness. It goes ahead of us, pointing toward a new and yet unrealized future of liberation whose dimensions are continually expanding as we become more sensitive to injustices which were overlooked in past cultures. Liberationists would use the prophetic tradition as the norm to critique the sexism of the religious tradition. Biblical sexism is not denied, but it loses its authority. It must be denounced as a failure to measure up to the full vision of human liberation of the prophetic and gospel messages.

A third group, we mentioned earlier, feel that women waste their time salvaging positive elements of these religious traditions. They take the spokesmen of patriarchal religion at their word when they say that Christ and God are literally and essentially male, and conclude that these religions have existed for no other purpose except to sanctify male domination. Women should quit the Church and the Synagogue and move to the feminist coven to celebrate the sacrality of women through recovery of the religion of the Goddess.

Although I myself am most sympathetic to the second view, I would regard all these positions as having elements of truth. All respond to real needs of different constituencies of women (and some men). It is unlikely that any of these views will predominate, but all will work as parallel trends in the ensuing decades to reshape the face of religion.

The evangelical feminists address themselves to an important group in American religion who frequently use Scripture to reinforce traditional patriarchal family models. Evangelical feminists wish to lift up neglected traditions and to give Biblicist Christians a basis for addressing the question of equality. They will probably get the liberal wing of these churches to modify their language and exegesis. The first creation story of women's and man's equal creation in the image of God will be stressed, rather than the second creation story of Eve from Adam's rib. Galatians 3, 28 will be stressed in Paul rather than Ephesians 5, and so forth. They might get some denominations to use inclusive language for the community and maybe even for God.

The liberationist wing would want Churches to take a much more active and prophetic role in critiquing the sexism of society, not only on such issues as abortion rights, gay rights and the ERA, but also on the links between sexism and economic injustice. They would press churches with a social gospel tradition into new questions about the adequacy of a patriarchal, capitalist, and consumerist economy to promote a viable human future.

The impact of the separatist goddess religions is more difficult to predict. Traditional Jews and Christians would view these movements as "paganism," if not "satanism." The Goddess movements are likely to respond in a equally defensive way and to direct their feelings against feminists who are still working within Churches and Synagogues. A lot depends on whether some mediating ground can be developed. On the one side, there would have to be a conscious rejection of the religious exclusivism of the Jewish and Christian traditions and a recognition of the appropriateness of experiencing the divine through female symbols and body images. The Goddess worshippers, in turn, might have to grow out of some of their defensiveness toward their Jewish and Christian sisters and start thinking about how we are to create a more comprehensive faith for our sons, as well as our daughters.

This is not to be construed as a call for such feminists to become (or return) to Judaism or Christianity, but rather a growth toward that kind of maturity that can recognize the legitimacy of religious quests in several kinds of contexts. As long as "goddess" feminists can only affirm their way by a reversed exclusivism and denial of the possibility of liberating elements in the Biblical tradition, they are still tied to the same exclusivist patterns of thought in an opposite form.

A creative dialogue between these two views could be very significant. Counter-cultural feminist spirituality could make important contributions to the enlargement of our religious symbols and experiences. We might be able to experience God gestating the world in Her womb, rather than just "making it" through a divine phallic fiat. We would rediscover the rhythms that tie us biologically with earth, fire, air and water which have been so neglected in our anti-natural spiritualities. We would explore the sacralities of the repressed parts of our psyches and our environmental experiences. Many worlds that have been negated by patriarchal religion might be reclaimed for the enlargement of our common life.

It is not clear what all this might mean. It might well be the beginning of a new religion as momentous in its break with the past as Christianity was with the religions of the Semites and the

Greeks. But if it is truly to enlarge our present options, it must also integrate the best of the insights that we have developed through Judaism and Christianity, as these religions integrated some (not all) of the best insights of the Near Eastern and Greco-Roman worlds. What is clear is this: the patriarchal repression of women and women's experience has been so massive and prevalent that to begin to take women seriously will involve a profound and radical transformation of our religions.

WHAT THE WOMEN'S MOVEMENT HAS DONE TO AMERICAN HISTORY

CARL N. DEGLER

ALTHOUGH MOST PEOPLE SEEM to think of the past as fixed and unchanging, much like a landscape, historians are more likely to see it as a seascape in which the scene is constantly changing and shifting. For the past does alter as we uncover new evidence from our rummaging through archives or stumbling upon sources not known to have existed before. It alters even more as we ask new questions of the past when our present-day concerns demand a new history. This, for example, is what happened when the place of black people in our society was a live issue in the 1950s and 1960s. A new impetus was thereby given to the study of slavery in the United States, the result of which was the greatest outpouring of historical research on a single topic in all of American historiography. In sum, the very definition of the past is continually being altered.

One of the most recent redefinitions of the content of the American past has been the new history of women. That this burgeoning interest in women's past is directly related to the modern women's movement can come as no surprise, for just as the new self-consciousness among blacks in the 1960s required a history, so the new consciousness among women has demanded nothing less. Only through history can a cause, or an issue, or a social group gain an identity, a sense of who or what it is.

The modern interest in women has reshaped the discipline of history in a variety of ways. Perhaps the most obvious has been to

Carl N. Degler, who earned his M.A. and Ph.D. at Columbia University, is Margaret Byrne Professor of American History at Stanford University. In 1972 he won the Pulitzer Prize in History for his book *Neither Black Nor White*. His most recent book, *At Odds: Women and the Family in America from the Revolution to the Present*, was published in Spring, 1980, by Oxford University Press.

require historians to rethink some of their old formulations of the past or their explanations for events and developments. Nowhere has this necessity to reexamine old explanations been more evident than in regard to an old chestnut of American history, namely, the frontier thesis of Frederick Jackson Turner. As David Potter pointed out some years before there was a serious women's movement, Turner's depiction of the frontier and its influence was quite sexist.[1] All of the characteristics that Turner ascribed to Americans, because they had to conquer a wilderness, actually applied to men only. It was men, after all, who, according to Turner, became individualistic because of their access to open land; it was men who became competitive because of their new opportunities; it was men who felt the egalitarianism spawned by a new land. Women, on the other hand, usually found their lives limited by the frontier; they made no fortunes from the land, or from a successful gold discovery, or by using the open federal lands to raise cattle. Rather, they were left at home to care for children and household; the empty land that provided the legendary opportunities for men worked a quite opposite effect upon women. It denied them an alternative to marriage, family, and home, for where would a woman go and how would she live if she left her traditional role as wife and mother? The truly devastating implications that the inclusion of women in history has for Turner's frontier thesis become blindingly clear if one notices the different responses of men and women to the ending of the frontier and the transformation of America into a nation of cities. In Turner's view, when the frontier closed a new era opened for Americans—for now they were dependent upon employers for their bread, lived under constrained circumstances in crowded cities, and obviously lost the opportunities implicit in the open land of the frontier. Turner, of course, did not recognize that he was talking only about men, for if he had, then he would have recognized that for women, the city had quite a different meaning. For women the city was opportunity, as the frontier never had been. In an urban environment women can earn their own living, as they could not, usually, in the wilderness or out on the plains. For the first time, they could be economically independent of men. It is not accidental that women have always been more numerous than men in cities, but always less numerous on the frontier.

The new interest in women's history has caused historians not only to rethink the meaning of old interpretations like Turner's, but also to begin to look into what the lives of women were like on the frontier, instead of either ignoring them or assuming that their experiences were the same as men's. John Faragher's *Women and Men on the Overland Trail* (1979) has tried to measure the differential impact of the overland experience on the two genders, something that would not have been done twenty years ago, although the sources have been there all along. What was required, of course, was a raising of consciousness or sensitivity to the existence of women in the past. As might be expected, Faragher's book is not alone. At just about the time he published his book on women in the West, Julie Roy Jeffrey issued hers.[2] Considerably broader—though briefer—than Faragher's, Jeffrey's book discusses, among other subjects, the position of women among the Mormons in nineteenth-century Utah. During the last century, the Latter Day Saints and their practice of polygyny were a major controversy, not least among women and their supporters. And today the usual conception of the Mormons is that they are not only hostile to the women's movement, but they also constrict women's social position. But, as Jeffrey's fine book shows, our conception of women in Mormon Utah may have to be reshaped in the light of the new research that has been spawned by the modern women's movement. One consequence of reopening a historical question is that we see a new past because new evidence has been discovered, and also because we now have new eyes, that is, a new sensitivity, with which to examine the past.

This has been happening in regard to the Revolution as well as the West. The era of the American Revolution has been and continues to be studied intensively, and properly so, since it is the founding event of the nation. But only since the women's movement has come into prominence has the role of women in it been canvassed with any concentration by professional historians. At the risk of oversimplification, it can be said that two recent books by Linda Kerber and Mary Beth Norton discern in the Revolution a significant turning point in the history of women in America.[3] The experience of the Revolution helped women achieve a new and better place in the family as well as a sense of having a political—albeit private, rather than public—role to play in the new Republic. Both Kerber and Norton, it is worth noting, entered the historical profession writing about the same eras in American history, but neither of them wrote her first book on the subject of women. It is not being audacious to conclude that it was the women's movement, which intervened between their first and second books, that directed their attention to the subjects they have most recently treated.

Not only women have been sensitized by the women's movement to recognize for the first time the presence of women in the past. Donald Matthews, in his important study of religion in the South, has called attention to the role of women in shaping the character of the Protestant churches in the South as no one has done before, even though, like the Revolution, religion has been a staple of historical inquiry. It was women, Matthews forthrightly asserts, who "made southern Evangelicalism possible." Not only were women the majority of church members, he pointed out, but "they provided indispensable support to the clergy. Almost every Methodist circuit rider and itinerant Baptist missionary who left an account of his work revealed an impressive reliance upon women for moral support as well as for basic physical comfort."[4] Less commendatory, but no less alert to the influence of women, is the conclusion reached by Ann Douglas in her *Feminization of American Culture* (1977). In that book, Douglas traces the strong influence of women not only on the Protestant ministers of the antebellum years, but also on the intellectual character of early nineteenth-century America. As her title suggests, Douglas locates the sources of what she considers the soft, rigorless, intellectual culture of our own time in the excessive influences of early-nineteenth-century women and sentimental ministers.

Probably no subject has been more reshaped by the new interest in women's place in modern America than that of women's suffrage. Until a decade ago, the winning of women's suffrage in 1919, with the adoption of the Nineteenth Amendment, was generally viewed as the final achievement of women's emancipation. If women entered the standard history texts of the nation, that was the time when they did; the achievement of the suffrage was usually perceived as one of several examples of successful Progressive reforms. But if gaining the suffrage by women marked the attainment of women's freedom, as so many history textbooks assured us, how did it come about that toward the end of the 1960s, a new women's movement erupted? That was the question William O'Neill raised in his *Everyone Was*

Brave: The Rise and Fall of Feminism in America (1969). O'Neill's answer was that the suffrage had not offered any real solution to the question of women's emancipation, for the oppression of women was a function of the patriarchal family, and that institution had not been touched by the suffrage. Hence, a new feminist movement had arisen to accomplish what the first had failed to do.

In O'Neill's view the feminist movement of the nineteenth century had been sidetracked into making the suffrage a central agency of women's emancipation and thus had redefined the woman's question in a way that obscured rather than exposed the root of women's subordination, namely, the patriarchal family. In O'Neill's analysis, then, the suffrage emerged as a rather minor achievement, perhaps something that should not have been pursued at all since the relation of husband and wife ought to have received the full attention of women activists. O'Neill's suggestion that the character of the family should have been the object of feminist agitation came in for harsh criticism. The critics pointed out that, in the nineteenth century, to call for alteration in the family was so radical as to be utopian. To have asked for equality between the sexes within the family was so extreme that O'Neill's analysis could easily be ignored as irrelevant or unrealistic. Yet, in the long term, he was quite correct. Only through a change in the family in the direction of greater autonomy or freedom for women would true emancipation be achieved. But to have expected that to be a realistic goal for the fledgling woman's movement of the late nineteenth century was indeed asking a little too much. In sum, O'Neill's understanding of the basic issue was sound enough, but his expectations for a solution were rather unrealistic.

The second line of criticism directed at O'Neill's book was more to the point. It recognized that the suffrage may have been oversold by the feminists, as O'Neill contended, but contrary to the implication in O'Neill's book, the suffrage was neither a minor nor a dispensable reform. The whole question of the historical meaning of suffrage was strikingly transformed when Ellen Du Bois, in a penetrating article, showed how radical the vote was for women.[5] Her point was that in the context of women's roles in nineteenth-century society, the suffrage was truly radical. It called into question all the traditional activities of women. It not only gave women the opportunity to act in politics, something that had almost always been denied them before, but it also recognized them as individuals within the family, something that the anti-suffragists and society in general also denied. In the traditional or patriarchal family a woman had been expected to subordinate her individual interests to those of her family. Thus a husband could quite properly represent his wife at the polls, because a woman's interests were no different from those of her husband. (The truly radical character of the suffrage had been obscured for O'Neill and other historians, because, when women did obtain the suffrage after 1920, they did not usually exercise it individualistically, that is, in pursuit of their own interests, as contrasted with those of their husbands. Today, of course, in the midst of a new feminist era, women often do vote their individual interests, and the results are to be seen in the increased number of women legislators, county executives, and mayors.)

Until the 1970s the standard historical interpretation of the so-called protective labor legislation enacted for women during the Progressive era at the opening of the twentieth century had been that such legislation was a sterling example of the way Progressivism and the women's movement of the time worked together toward common goals. Under the impact of the modern women's movement, that interpretation has been virtually reversed. The shining example of the cooperation between women and the progressive leaders was the famous legal brief that Louis D. Brandeis, the well-known Progressive lawyer and later Supreme court justice, presented to the United States Supreme Court and which, in the case of *Muller v. Oregon* in 1908, culminated in the landmark decision. In the brief, which Brandeis had drawn up with the assistance of several women labor activists, he argued that women's hours of work and conditions and character of labor could be constitutionally defined by law, because, as potential mothers, women workers deserved protections the law could not constitutionally give to male workers. Throughout the early years of the twentieth century, friends of women pushed for such laws in the states with notable success. So important did protective labor legislation appear to most women leaders that, when Alice Paul in 1923 proposed an Equal Rights Amendment to the United States Constitution, she and it were denounced by most feminist leaders because the Amendment would overturn all the protective legislation of the previous two decades. The ERA continued to be rejected by the great majority of women activists until the 1970s, when a new feminist movement asserted an individualist, rather than a collectivist, approach to women's work. Today, protective labor legislation is considered to be retrogressive, a limitation on women as individuals. Thus a movement once thought by historians—female as well as male—as a social gain, is today seen, thanks to the women's movement, as a detour, if not a roadblock on the path to women's full emancipation.

The temperance movement and its culmination, Prohibition, have also been reassessed, thanks to the influence of the modern woman's movement. Historians have not been kind in their treatment of temperance or Prohibition. In fact, Americans in general seem to be rather ashamed of that episode in their history. Although most people would concede that all historical experiences deserve to be seen in their own terms, temperance and Prohibition, in a society that treasures its alcoholic pleasures, have been difficult to see objectively. Today, however, historians of women are much more appreciative of the temperance movement, if only because they recognize the large role played by women in it. They recognize that women's heavy participation was a reflection of the impact liquor had upon the home, an institution in which women in the nineteenth century were centrally involved and upon which they were dependent. It helps to explain, too, why the Women's Christian Temperance Union was a much larger women's organization than any suffrage group was to be until the eve of ratification of the Nineteenth Amendment. Historians, it is true, have long been interested in accounting for the triumph of national prohibition in 1919 with the ratification of the Eighteenth Amendment. But they have been quite remiss in not taking seriously the role of women in bringing about Prohibition, although any objective study of that event would make evident the important place of women in its accomplishment.[6]

The coming of Prohibition is an example of how women's role in the American past has been ignored by historians when they seek to account for changes. A related but different way our thinking about the American past is transformed when we are conscious of women in the past, can be observed when we examine the social decision to open education to girls. There have been a number of studies of the struggle to provide access for young women to higher education, it is true. But that was a battle, something that always attracts the attention of historians. If one looks at the American past from the standpoint of women, another aspect of educational history cries out for attention. It is the decision to include girls in primary and secondary schooling on a par with boys.

The results of the social decision to include girls are striking. We do not know as much about the extent of literacy in early America as we would like, but it seems clear that on the eve of the Revolution literacy among men was quite high; perhaps as many as 80 percent of all adult males could at least write their names. So far as we can tell, the rate for adult women, even in highly literate New England, was no more than half that of men, or about 40 percent. Though there was a long tradition of education in the New England colonies and some others as well, girls were never included within it. If a girl learned to read and write, it was because a parent thought it desirable; public policy did not push in that direction at all. Yet, if we examine literacy rates in the middle of the nineteenth century, the different rates for the two sexes have disappeared. In their place is a single rate for both sexes—about 91–94 percent for adults, even for those living in rural areas.[7]

Because so much of historical thinking up until the modern women's movement has been concerned with men, this shift in attitude and behavior has simply not been studied. Although one may make some intelligent guesses as to what happened to bring women's literacy rate up to that of men, we really do not yet have any systematic study of the question. Yet it is clear that when publicly supported education began to spread from city to city and from state to state in the course of the nineteenth century, almost invariably it was decided (or assumed?) that girls as well as boys would be included in the school house. Moreover, segregation by gender has been rare in American public education from the beginning. Again, we must ask, why? Now that we are self-consciously looking at women in our past we may begin to find out.

Change in family fertility is another aspect of American history in which, surprising as it may sound, women have been ignored when explanations have been sought. For some time now, demographers have known that between 1800 and 1900 the fertility of white American families dropped 50 percent. Since the fertility of Americans during the colonial period had been among the highest in the eighteenth-century world, that deep fall in the nineteenth century calls for explanation. Why did Americans suddenly decide, in the opening years of the nineteenth century, to cut back on the size of their families? One might expect that women, since they bear and usually rear children, would have been seen as playing a significant role in bringing about this change. Yet few demographers have seriously considered them as decision-makers in even this respect.[8] More recently, however, historians interested in the place of women in the American past have been emphasizing the special interest (and autonomy) women have had in exerting some control over their fertility.[9] Not only do they have the same interests as men in cutting family costs, they also have an interest in reducing their own responsibilities for rearing children, not to mention their interest in reducing the risks to their lives in childbirth.

Changes in fertility suggest yet another way in which the recent women's movement has affected the writing of American history. Changes in fertility have long been a concern of demographers. Generally, in explaining those changes, as already observed, demographers have paid little or no attention to women as decision-makers. They have treated fertility as a masculine concern, that is, something which responds to the economic or social needs of men. But as women have been quick to point out, family fertility may be a male concern, but it is surely a female problem, if only because women have to bear the children. And because they bear the children, women historians have been alerted to the place of sexuality in history.

Sex is to women's history as color is to black history. Both are sources of differentiation and therefore a possible basis for differential treatment by those with power. But if one follows this line of thinking, it is evident that sex or gender is more than simply a source of difference between men and women; it is also a relation, a basis of cooperation as well as of conflict. Moreover, the most common form of that relation—marriage—is also the primary basis for women's subordination. Given the importance of sexuality in women's subordination, it is not to be wondered that since the emergence of the modern women's movement, sexuality has become an accepted subject among historians. There are even some indications that the sexuality of men may also be a subject of historical inquiry as time passes.

The historical analysis of women's sexuality has been approached from a variety of angles. Some historians have been intent upon setting forth the image of sex in the past, while others have tried to make a distinction between image and behavior, contending that the image cannot be assumed to reflect actual behavior. And from what we have learned about the behavior of women sexually and from their discussions of sex in their letters and diaries, it is evident that images are not good guides to behavior whatever they may tell us about social ideals or expectations. Still other historians have been aware that sexuality is more than simply a relation between men and women. The work of Carroll Smith-Rosenberg has been particularly influential in its depiction and analysis of "love and ritual" between women in the nineteenth century.[10] Her work has been a stimulus not only to the history of sexuality, but to the history of families, as well.

Smith-Rosenberg merely suggested that lesbianism may have been an aspect of some of these relations between women, but Lillian Faderman has more recently pressed the point in a powerful book.[11] Suddenly the term "Boston marriage" has become a part of our vocabulary in describing relations between women of the nineteenth century. Again, it is undoubtedly the new women's movement that has opened our eyes to an aspect of our past long obscured by the male orientation of almost all written history, even among many women historians in the past.

One significant consequence of seeing women as sexual beings as well as sexual objects is that the whole question of the nature of human sexuality is opened up afresh. Although there is no agreement among feminists or historians on the issue, and there probably will not be any for some time, it seems clear that when the history of the sexuality of the two sexes is studied systematically and fully, we will have a new understanding of this much discussed subject. We will be in a much better position to understand the *cultural* — as opposed to the biological — character of sexuality.

As one might expect, the question of sexuality in history has helped to make fertility-control and childbirth subjects of historical inquiry. Suddenly, thanks to the women's movement, those aspects of life that are peculiarly female, like child-bearing and child-rearing, are legitimate subjects of a historical study. Several books on child-bearing have already been published and undoubtedly more are on the way.[12] The way in which society views child-bearing obviously has relevance to the ways in which it perceives women, children, and families.

The question of the motives for the fall in fertility in the course of the nineteenth century may not have been answered as yet, but the search for an explanation as to *how* fertility was reduced has been somewhat more successful. At least four books have been published on various methods of birth control, including abortion. And though all but one of these books was written by a man, it is evident that the modern women's movement has been influential in stimulating all of them. David Kennedy focused his work on the leading woman advocate of birth control, Margaret Sanger, while James Reed in his history of contraception was clearly motivated by a personal concern for women's emancipation from unwanted pregnancies.[13] Linda Gordon's social history of birth control explicitly announced its feminist origins as well as its feminist orientation.[14] Even before the Supreme Court overthrew state laws against abortion, in the case of *Roe v. Wade* in 1973, abortion had become an important woman's issue. As a result, the history of abortion has been a topic of serious concern among historians, as shown by James Mohr's excellent volume *Abortion in America* (1978). What it and other studies of the subject reveal is that abortion came to the forefront as a method of fertility control only in the nineteenth century. As a peculiarly woman's method, abortion, once its incidence is socially significant, becomes a measure of women's interest in controlling their own fertility, especially when men fail to cooperate in asserting that control. Although by the second half of the nineteenth century almost all states had made abortions illegal and no women leaders of the time supported abortion, the high incidence of abortion among married women is a revealing gauge of the determination of ordinary women to limit their fertility.

A recognition that women were indeed a part of the past results not only in new subjects being included in formal history, or in old subjects being reinterpreted. It also causes historians to devise fresh methods for analyzing the past. Some historians and sociologists, it is true, have contended that women are no more than a special kind of minority, and minorities have been studied for some time. Women, to be sure, constitute 50 percent or more of the population, but if one uses the word "minority" in the sense that it implies lack of social power, then it is not illogical to consider women as a minority. Certainly that was the point that sociologist Helen Hacker made a number of years ago in a much discussed article in which, point by point, she demonstrated the similarity between the history and modern position of women and those of an acknowledged minority group like blacks. Both have been denied equal access to education at some point in their histories, both have been seen as social subordinates, both have been excluded from political participation, both have been assigned social places from which they must not depart, and both have been excluded from certain jobs.[15]

Admittedly, there are important advantages to be gained from seeing women as a minority, but no sooner does one try to fit them into such a conceptualization than one is forced to recognize the limitations of the idea. Women as a social group are *sui generis*, they cannot be studied as if they were just another social group. In fact, some social historians have been so impressed by the special character of women in society that they deny there is any such thing as a history of women. Professor Eugen Weber, of the University of California at Los Angeles, recently made just that point when he told a reporter that he personally found "a difference between a history of Chicanos, for example, and a history of women. Ethnic groups are distinct societies, at least for a time, but women and men operate in symbiosis, not separate from the rest of society."[16] If the only groups that can be studied in the past are those which have a existence distinct from the dominant group, then it follows that women do not have a history. But if one defines history as experience, then there does not seem to be any reason why women are not as legitimate a part of history as Chicanos or any other group that has what Weber calls "distinct societies." Yet, there is a truth hidden in Weber's remark that must be acknowledged if we are to appreciate the extent of the need for a new way of looking at the past now that women are included.

Women, in truth, are like minorities, as Hacker and others have pointed out, but they are also, as Weber implied, quite different, for they are a sex. This difference between women and all other minorities can be put in a more concrete, if more paradoxical, way than Weber did. The standard measure of the acceptance of a minority by a majority in any society, sociologists tell us, is the degree to which the minority is able to intermarry with the ruling group. Insofar as women are concerned, that test not only fails to apply, its reversal is closer to the truth. Intermarriage by women with the master class (men) is actually the principal source of women's oppression, not a sign of their acceptance.

Because women are a sex, there is another way in which they differ importantly from minorities. Unlike all other minorities, women are spread throughout the social structure, which is another way of saying that they are divided—as men are—by class. Minorities, on the other hand, are usually *united* by class, since they generally are concentrated at the bottom of the social structure. In a sense, of course, that is Weber's point when he refers to women as having a symbiotic relation with men; women are very likely to have their identity as women obscured by their class differences. And that, in turn, helps us to understand why the women's movement, both today and in the past, has had a difficult time uniting all classes of women in a common movement. Thus, if one is going to study the place of women in the past, new ways of thinking and writing about them will have to be devised just because class divisions create barriers among groups of women as well as prescribing different life styles. At the same time, just because the essential problem for women is their relation to men, there are common patterns of behavior that transcend differences of class. Within families, for example, regardless of class, the preponderance of power has been in the hands of father or husband.

Concern with the relations of power within the family, however, should not lead us to think that analyzing power relations between women and men is the same as between other superiors and inferiors. Superficially, slaves, employees, and women seem to have something in common since all are subordinates. Yet even the most cursory acquaintance with the relation between husband and wife makes it clear that there are significant differences between that relation and those experienced by other subordinates. First of all, women usually have a choice in choosing their superiors—we call it courting—something slaves and employees generally do not have. Second, women have a source of power over their husbands through the sexual/love feelings from which the relation between them derives. A woman may use the affection her husband has for her as a lever with which she can obtain something she wants. Obviously, there are limits to this source of power, but affection offers an opportunity for a wife that no slave nor employee enjoys—unless the slave or employee is a female, of course. Finally, the children which women share with their husbands provide women with an additional basis for protecting their interests that no other subordinates enjoy. In sum, if one is going to talk about women as subordinates, and certainly one ought to if one's analysis is going to be realistic, then we need to recognize that in such a situation they are *sui generis,* too. We need a fresh and more imaginative way of defining their subordination than simply drawing on what we know about the subordination of slaves or workers.

That this is a real and perhaps pressing need is shown by some of the recent writings about the meaning of woman's place in nineteenth-century America. Just because the women of the middle class were confined to the home and excluded from most of the activities of the public world, many scholars have defined marriage or domesticity in the past century as not only a position of subordination, but one that constituted a decline in women's status. Domesticity in the writings of Carroll Smith-Rosenberg, for example, has usually been equated with such a high degree of subordination as to be considered a source of women's illness as well as a source of frustration.[17] On the other hand, some other historians, notably Nancy Cott[18] and Julie Roy Jeffrey, have recognized that in a number of ways domesticity within the context of the early nineteenth century may have been not only an improvement in the status of women, but an occupation that fitted fairly comfortably within the interests and purposes of women at that time. In short, there is a danger of being anachronistic by interpreting the meaning of women's lives in the nineteenth century by the standards of the twentieth. Domesticity was not so much a prison as a way-station on the road to greater autonomy. Again, it means disenthralling our thinking when we treat women in history.

Probably nothing has demonstrated more clearly the way in which the emergence of women's studies has required a rethinking of old ways of doing history than the effect the women's movement has had on Marxist thought. Although in theory Marxists have long been in favor of equality between the sexes, in practice there has not been much of it, as we learn from some of the recent work by radical women. Indeed, it is a cliché of the women's movement that during the 1960s many young radical women first became active feminists when they recognized they were being treated as subordinates by their self-proclaimed egalitarian male colleagues in the civil rights movement. Nowhere was the attitude more obvious than in Stokely Carmichael's famous retort to the question of what was the position of women in the movement. "Prone," was Carmichael's quick sexist response.[19]

In the late 1970s many radical and Marxist women began to reexamine Marxist theory, because suddenly it was evident that the class analysis of Marxism could not really handle the problem of how to create an equal relation between the sexes. Or as economist Heidi Hartmann has put the matter: "Recent attempts to integrate Marxism and feminism are unsatisfactory to us as feminists because they subsume the feminist struggle into the 'larger' struggle against capital."[20] To women recently sensitized by the women's movement, it was no longer axiomatic that once capitalism was overthrown gender inequalities would also be overthrown. The early Marxists, Hartmann continued, "did not focus on the feminist questions—how and why women are opposed as women. They did not . . . recognize the vested interest men had in women's continued subordination."[21] As a result, today a number of radical and Marxist women are struggling to reshape Marxist theory to fit feminist needs and aspirations.

Finally, as a way of suggesting how the new concern for women in present and past society has reshaped the study of history, mention may be made of the new Feminist Studies major that has been organized at Stanford University. Despite the title, the new program is not feminist in the sense that it advocates feminism, but in the sense that it moves beyond merely women's studies. As a new field of inquiry, women's studies has called attention to the place of women in a variety of disciplines running from history, sociology, and anthropology to English, art, and philosophy. But, as the proponents of the new feminist studies point out, in the end, women's studies are concerned only with those aspects of life in which women have played a part. Thus women's studies usually has little or nothing to do with military, or political history, for instance, because, on the average, women have not been involved in those activities, at least in the past. Feminist studies, on the other hand, seeks to broaden the whole matter by asking the general question of *any* sphere of activity: what difference did it make that women were included or were not included in those activities? And if they were not included, why were they not? Thus feminist studies constitutes yet another example of how the emergence of women's concerns in the last quarter of the twentieth century has caused historians (and others) to think creatively as well as critically about what they are doing and how they do it.

If there is little doubt that the new interest in women in society has sparked new thinking by historians about their craft and their ways of pursuing it, a good deal of doubt remains that the principal reason for examining the history of women is being realized. The ultimate aim, after all, is to have women included in the history of the nation, not simply to have them studied by themselves. Virtually all of the examples provided in this essay have concerned the history of women, not history in general. The significant development will occur among historians when women are included in the general history of the United States. So far, it has to be admitted, little tangible progress has been made toward that important goal. A number of college textbooks, it is true, now mention or discuss women to an extent not known ten years ago; a few more famous women are pictured or described, and perhaps more paragraphs are devoted to women in the workplace than before. But the shape of the American past, that is to say, the structure through which we pass on our history to students, has remained almost unchanged. Yet if we are to include women in our past we will clearly have to rethink what we mean by our past, if only because history as it has been written over the last several hundred years has been the story of what men have done. That is why history has been heavily concerned with politics, foreign affairs, economics, business, military activities, and government. Those have been the concerns of men, and the men in those institutions and activities have wanted a history of them. This means that the content and the divisions—periodization historians call it—of history are largely determined now by the interests of men. This is not to suggest that there was some grand conspiracy to exclude women from history, for that is not the best way of describing the matter. Better to say that because men have dominated society, the history they found most useful was that which depicted the activities and institutions that interested them. But if today we are to have a history that is useful to both men and women, then we will have to recast our past to accommodate the history of both. It may well involve different periodization, different content, and different emphases. In the end there is only one history, not two or three. In an integrated, egalitarian society, which is what I think we aspire to today, we can have only integrated history.

To date, the efforts to work out an integrated history have not borne much fruit. Several conferences have been held under the auspices and funding of the National Endowment for the Humanities to work out syllabi in American and European history toward this end, but they have been no more than experimental. The effort continues because the purpose is sound. Professor Gerda Lerner of the University of Wisconsin has personally dedicated herself to producing a theory of women's history which seeks to place that subject on the level with the history we have known up to now. Her theoretical insights may well provide novel ways of integrating women's history with traditional history. But, again, the consummation is still in the future.

The most important point of all is that any new, integrated history must be truly composite and not one-sided. It must not be simply history written from the standpoint of women. That will not serve the purposes of men, who also need history, however much such one-sided women's history may right the imbalance from which traditional history has suffered for so long. If women's history is to serve women—as it certainly is intended to do—then it must make women's past a part of the story of humankind's experience. Such a new history will certainly mean restructuring the past as well as interpreting it, and perhaps seeing other meanings for the present than we do now. It will also undoubtedly mean eliminating many things once thought indispensable, but that will not be a new activity for historians. Although the achievement of such a history may be difficult and lengthy in accomplishment, it is worth attempting, because only through a common past can all people relate to one another, and understand who they are as well as where they have come from. With an integrated history, women as well as men will attain historical depth.

84

NOTES

1. David M. Potter, "American Women and the American Character," *Stetson University Bulletin*, LXII (January, 1962), 1-22.
2. Julie Roy Jeffrey, *Frontier Women: The Trans-Mississippi West, 1840-1880* (New York: Hill and Wang, 1979).
3. Linda K. Kerber, *Women of the Republic: Intellect and Ideology in Revolutionary America* (Chapel Hill: University of North Carolina Press, 1980); Mary Beth Norton, *Liberty's Daughters: The Revolutionary Experience of American Women, 1750-1800* (Boston: Little Brown, 1980).
4. Donald G. Mathews, *Religion in the Old South* (Chicago: University of Chicago Press, 1977), p. 102.
5. Ellen Du Bois, "The Radicalism of the Women Suffrage Movement: Notes Toward the Reconstruction of Nineteenth-Century Feminism," *Feminist Studies*, 3 (Fall, 1975), 63-71.
6. See, for example, Ross Evans Paulson, *Women's Suffrage and Prohibition: A Comparative Study of Equality and Social Control* (Glenview, Ill.: Scott, Foresman, 1973) and Ruth Bordin, *Woman and Temperance: The Quest for Power and Liberty, 1873-1900* (Philadelphia: Temple University Press, 1981).
7. Richard A. Easterlin, "Factors in the Decline of Farm Family Fertility in the United States: Some Preliminary Research Results," *Journal of American History*, LXIII (December, 1976), 602, 608.
8. See, for example, Yasukichi Yasuba, *Birth Rates of the White Population in the United States, 1800-1860* (Baltimore: Johns Hopkins University Press, 1961).
9. Daniel Scott Smith, "Family Limitation, Sexual Control, and Domestic Feminism in Victorian America," in Mary S. Hartman and Lois W. Banner, eds., *Clio's Consciousness Raised* (New York: Harper Torchbooks, 1974) and Carl N. Degler, *At Odds: Women and the Family in America from the Revolution to the Present* (New York: Oxford University Press, 1980), Chapter VIII.
10. Carroll Smith-Rosenberg, "The Female World of Love and Ritual: Relations between Women in Nineteenth-Century America," *Signs*, I (Autumn, 1975), 1-29.
11. Lillian Faderman, *Surpassing the Love of Man; Romantic Friendship and Love between Women from the Renaissance to the Present* (New York: William Morrow, 1981).
12. Catherine M. Scholten, "On the importance of the Obstetrick Art: Changing Customs of Childbirth in America, 1760-1825," *William and Mary Quarterly* 3rd Series, 34 (July, 1977), 426–45; Judy Barrett Litoff, *American Midwives: 1860 to the Present* (Westport, Conn.: Greenwood Press, 1978).
13. David M. Kennedy, *Birth Control in America: The Career of Margaret Sanger* (New Haven: Yale University Press, 1970); James Reed, *From Private Vice to Public Virtue: The Birth Control Movement and American Society Since 1830* (New York: Basic Books, 1978).
14. Linda Gordon, *Woman's Body, Woman's Rights: A Social History of Birth Control in America* (New York: Gross Publishers, 1976).
15. Helen Hacker, "Women as a Minority Group," *Social Forces* XXX (October, 1951), 60–69.
16. *Los Angeles Times*, April 23, 1981.
17. Carroll Smith-Rosenberg, "The Hysterical Woman: Sex Roles and Role Conflict in 19th Century America," *Social Research*, XLIX (Winter, 1972), 652–78.

18. Nancy F. Cott, *The Bonds of Womanhood: "Woman's Sphere" in New England, 1780-1835* (New Haven: Yale University Press, 1977).

19. Quoted in William Henry Chafe, *The American Woman: Her Changing Social, Economic, and Politic Roles, 1920-1970* (New York: Oxford University Press, 1972), p. 233.

20. Heidi Hartmann, "The Unhappy Marriage of Marxism and Feminism: Towards a More Progressive Union," in Lydia Sargent, ed., *Women and Revolution* (South End Press, Boston, 1981), p. 2.

21. *Ibid.*, p. 5.

SPEAKING FROM SILENCE:
Women and the Science of Politics

NANNERL O. KEOHANE

BEFORE THE EARLY 1970s, references to women in the academic study of politics were rare. Few standard works of scholarship took notice of sex as a relevant variable, and even fewer discussed it seriously, rather than dismissing it with an uninformed and superficial paragraph. The handful of articles and books explicitly devoted to women in politics seldom appeared on reading lists for courses in the discipline. In late 1974, three articles appeared simultaneously calling attention to this set of facts. The authors of one article regarded it as a "safe prediction" that more would be learned about women and politics in the 1970s than in all previous decades of the history of the discipline combined.[1]

This prediction has been handsomely borne out. In that same year (1974), two important books on women in politics were published.[2] They have been followed by other studies, with increasing frequency and variety, in subsequent years. It is no longer uncommon to discover an article about women in politics when one opens a major journal in the field; several have devoted special issues or symposia to the topic.[3] In 1980, a journal specifically entitled *Women and Politics* appeared for the first time. Taken together, these resources have advanced our understanding enormously, compared with the state of the art in 1974. And since increasing numbers of scholars regard women in politics as a promising area for research, there is good reason to expect the upward trend to be maintained.

Nannerl O. Keohane, educated at Wellesley, Oxford, and Yale, has been a professor of political science at Swarthmore College and Stanford University. She is the author of *Philosophy and the State: The Renaissance to the Enlightenment* (Princeton 1980), as well as several articles on political theory and feminist scholarship. In July 1981 she became President of Wellesley College.

However, the volume of published work is still meagre, as a proportion of scholarship in the discipline. The development of a body of material sufficient to provide a scholarly subdisciplinary community with a sense of purpose and cohesion is still in the early stages. More sobering, attention to women remains an isolated corner of the field and has so far had little impact on the discipline as a whole, compared with sister disciplines. In women's studies, a good piece of conventional wisdom holds that it is not enough simply to "add women and stir." In political science, women are just now being added, and the field has hardly begun to stir.

Why has the study of politics lagged so far behind other social sciences on this score? And how can we expect the discipline to be altered by the growing attention to women and politics in the future?

I. Normal politics: Male dominance

The public realm, across cultures and over the centuries, has been male-centered to an extent unparalleled in other parts of human social life. Virtually all offices charged with responsibility for making or carrying out decisions that affect an entire society have been held by men. Women have seldom exercised authority over groups containing men of equivalent age and social class. Anthropologists confirm the universality of this truth in different kinds of societies. As Shelly Rosaldo put it recently: "Women may have ritual powers of considerable significance to themselves as well as men, but women never dominate in rites requiring the participation of the community as a whole.... I know of no case where men are required to serve as an obligatory audience to female ritual of political performance."[4] Cabinets and legislatures, councils of diplomacy and commerce, assemblies and courts of justice have been almost exclusively populated by males and so, of course, have all the armies.

The near-monopoly of males in jural/executive and military/coercive offices in almost all societies is the first fact to keep in mind in considering the absence of women from the study of politics. Rather than constituting a satisfactory explanation in itself, however, this fact simply draws our attention to a host of problems requiring explanation. The first is: why should this radical asymmetry by sexes not itself have been a research problem of the first magnitude for the discipline throughout the years? Why, that is, was it consistently taken for granted that men and not women should populate the public sphere, and why did so few observers stop to meditate upon this fascinating fact?[5]

Secondly, what about the exceptions to the rule? There are women whose accomplishments in this area are legendary: Elizabeth and Deborah, Catherine and Cleopatra, Boadicea and Joan of Arc. Many others, thrust into public life by accident of royal blood or widowhood or extraordinary purpose, accomplished less and were more easily discounted. But all these women — famous, infamous and nonentities — have been ignored in the discipline of political science. The potentially fascinating set of questions about how a woman's way of exercising authority might differ from a man's has been almost totally neglected. So has the equally fascinating range of questions about what kinds of societies, or situations, or conceptions of the state, are most likely to provide occasion for the appearance of a woman ruler. The few scholars who observed women in power in the past were more concerned to warn against the "monstrous regiment of women" or speculate about the problems faced by a female prince in disposing her sexual favors without disturbing the equilibrium of the kingdom than to give systematic attention to the character of female rulership.[6] There is no pigeonhole in the science of politics comparable to "Abnormal Psychology" for dealing with this rich set of aberrant cases.

The ease with which discussions of women in authority have slipped into prurient diatribes about sexuality and power highlights yet another aspect of the problem. Whereas women are rarely found in official positions, a whole repertoire of more subtle ways of exercising power are conventionally attributed to women. The power of the beautiful woman in the boudoir and the clever woman in the salon, of the mother who stops at nothing to get power for her son, or the wife or mistress who exercises the power behind the throne — all these patterns of influence associated with women occasion suspicion, fear, ridicule or reluctant admiration. But they do not form part of the subject matter of the study of politics as it has developed since the Greeks.

Part of the explanation for the neglect of this range of female practices of power lies in the focus on public and authoritative, "legitimate" activities by academic students of politics. But shrewd observers of public life, including many who have contributed to the development of political science as a discipline, have often noticed other covert, arcane and "corrupt" practices and taken them into account in understanding politics. Private negotiations, bribery, log-rolling, the diverse forms of influence and manipulation have hardly gone unnoticed. But while we have a fairly good understanding of the traditional role of the *eminence grise,* we lack any comparable notion of the motivations and activities of the *eminence rose.* Lacking any vocabulary for discussing the intersection of sexuality and politics, or describing maternal or wifely strategies, students of politics have taken refuge in mutterings about inscrutability, irrationality, or hormones, and dismissed the power of womankind as an unpredictable force that has no place in a properly ordered political universe. As one Victorian authority on "Woman in Politics" announced, a woman is "not unlike a package of dynamite, perfectly harmless till some one disturbs the equilibrium of its particles, but then a power, the precise limit of which it is impossible to predict with accuracy."[7]

Finally, the academic study of politics has ignored the manifold ways in which authority is exercised, decisions are made, and the common good of a group of people is given over to the responsibility of a few in associations that form parts of "society" rather than the "state": corporations, convents, harems, universities, families, nursery schools and prisons, for example. By restricting its focus narrowly to the formal business of the state or the city and failing to take the exercise of authority in such associations as part of its province, the study of politics has systematically neglected those arenas in which women are most frequently found in authoritative roles.

For all these reasons, women have been—to use a word that writers on this topic often use—"invisible" in the study of politics. The participation of women, and even more strikingly their *non-participation,* in public life, have been classic non-issues for students of politics. Today, two major types of concurrent change are altering these conditions, although to what extent we cannot yet know. First, women are moving into positions of official authority, from town councils to prime ministries, in numbers without precedent in history. Understanding why this change is occurring at this time is itself a research challenge of exceptional importance, and the result of the change is a dramatic increase in the data base of women in office to be studied.

Another kind of change, largely (but not wholly) independent of the first, is taking place in the way the discipline of political science understands its subject matter.

Two opposed hypotheses can be advanced about the degree to which increased participation by women will alter the character of public life. The first holds that, after a brief period of adjustment, women in office will behave just like men, and the temper of public life will be fundamentally unchanged. Support for this null hypothesis can be found in the experience of Europe and America as the suffrage was gradually extended to the poor, the Blacks, the women, and the young. In each case dire predictions of social upset proved unfounded and the new groups were assimilated into old practices. Further support for the same hypothesis is given by the behavior of women leaders such as Margaret Thatcher or Indira Gandhi, which does not appear to differ from that of male counterparts along gender lines, even though their femaleness attracts notice by reason of its oddity. According to this hypothesis, any differences that may occur in female performance of political roles can be attributed to the general problems of tokenism rather than to any specific differences of female character.[8] The holding of office imposes certain attitudes and behaviors that will prove more important than any differences based on sex. Gender distinctions in public life will gradually become unimportant as women office-holders become more common.

The alternative hypothesis holds that as women become more numerous in public office, they will bring a distinctive set of traits and concerns that will begin to alter the character of public life. Whether this set of female traits is held to be rooted in some distinctively female "nature," given by biology and feminine psychology, or instead is the stubborn residue of centuries of differential socialization and cultural experience, in this view the influx of women will make a major difference in the practice of politics, and resistance to these changes may delay the full participation of women in public life for a long time. Proponents of this second hypothesis might point out that the assimilation of new social groups has often had a profound effect on the tenor and goals of public life, even if it is delayed for many generations. They are more likely, however, to argue that the difference between male and female is *sui generis* in quality and unparalleled in importance, so that evidence from prior assimilation of previously excluded social groups is not very pertinent.

Support for this second hypothesis can also be found by reaching outside the discipline of political science as it has been traditionally understood, and examining a whole range of differences between males and females in patterns of language use, interpersonal relations, handling violence, children's play, and fantasy. Feminist scholars have taken the lead in this adventurous broadening of the discipline's scope, but they have not been alone. Several contemporary modifications of the subject matter of political science are providing useful new tools and concepts for this extended inquiry. More and more political scientists, influenced by recent research in social history, psychology, sociology and economics, are paying attention to informal authority relationships, and studying the political dynamics of associations outside the sphere of public life as it has conventionally been defined. Scholars engaged in such research, even when they are not directly motivated by an interest in studying women, contribute to our understanding of non-traditional patterns of authority and suggest alternatives to the conception of "normal politics" that has been dominant for so long.[9]

On these grounds, it is possible to predict that attention to women in politics will make a substantial difference in the academic study of politics in the next few decades. To lend support to this prediction, I will consider some of the ways in which the discipline is already changing, and identify some trends that seem likely to ensure that these changes will continue.

II. Speech and silence

The magnitude of the task of bringing women into the subject matter of the science of politics is best appreciated if we recognize the power of the traditional taboos that have kept them out of public life. One especially pertinent way to describe these taboos is by using the language of speaking and silence. Speech, discourse, and voice have been effective metaphors for political activity since the Greeks. From Plato's creation of a "city in speech" in the *Republic,* through the power of the Hobbesian sovereign as the power of naming and controlling words, to Hannah Arendt's contemporary definition of speech as the central activity in a fully human life, and Albert Hirschman's metaphors of exit, *voice*, and loyalty, speech has been a central motif in human public life. In this context, the durable association of women and silence is especially revealing.

There are two aspects of the silence to which women are enjoined. First, women are instructed by the dominant tradition of moral philosophy in our culture to be silent in the presence of men. Silence is associated with modesty, purity, and woman's virtue. Aristotle quotes Sophocles approvingly: "A modest silence is a woman's crown."[10] The Pauline injunction against women speaking up in church is echoed down the centuries in this Victorian homily: "The true destiny of a woman is to wed a man she can love and esteem . . . and to lead *noiselessly*, under his protection, with all the wisdom, grace and heroism that is in her, the life presented in consequence."[11] (emphasis added) The power of such prescriptive silence is such that when women do speak, their speech sounds strange. It deviates from the norm of masculinity, in timbre and in pattern. Women's speech, as modern research in sociolinguistics makes clear, differs from men's speech.[12] And the words of women are consistently devalued in group settings, not heard, assumed to be trivial, not attended to.

But this is only half the difficulty. Not only is the norm across cultures and history that women should be silent, it is also held that they should not be spoken of by men. If a woman becomes an object of male discourse, it is probably because she has become a "public" woman in the sense used by Rousseau, the only sense he knew, a loose woman or a prostitute.[13] One aspect of the prominence of speech in western public life is extolling the deeds and singing the praises of noble heroes, so that the highest honor a man can hope for is to see his name become famous and a *topos* for discussion. For a woman, the opposite is true: the less heard of her, the more virtuous she must have been.

Pericles' great "Funeral Oration," as reconstructed by Thucydides, makes this parallel quite striking. His theme is the celebration of heroism and noble deeds, and the motif of speech is central to the discourse. At the very end, just before the benediction, Pericles remarks:

> On the other hand, if I must say anything on the subject of female excellence to those of you who will now be in widowhood, it will be all comprised in this brief exhortation: Great will be your glory in not

falling short of your natural character; and greatest will be hers who is least talked of among the men, whether for good or for bad.[14]

So much is imbedded in this brief passage. Women come to public notice only as widows of the glorious dead; the sole measure of female virtue is to be not-spoken-of. This is the natural character of women—one that they must strive to reach. And yet, behind the scenes, Greek women certainly were speaking, whether with the poetic power of a Sappho or the legendary political shrewdness of Pericles' own mistress, Aspasia, who was a prototype of what I have called the *eminence rose*. Why must we hear nothing of Aspasia? The search for Aspasia is one of the first tasks of a feminist science of politics; another, even more important, is paying attention to the voices of those who are part of what Kirsten Amundsen so aptly called "the silenced majority."[15] To what extent are these tasks already being carried out, and how?

III. The impact of women's studies on the study of politics

Two recent articles in the *News for Teachers of Political Science* offer specific, and parallel, suggestions for incorporating women into courses in political philosophy and American government.[16] Drawing on both essays, we can identify four different (not mutually exclusive) approaches available to political scientists who want to pay attention to women in their teaching and research.

First, and most obvious, is the inclusion of work by women political scientists in material used for teaching and for supportive evidence in research. The importance of this step is both symbolic and substantial. Seeing women's names cited more frequently accustoms all readers to expecting that women will be taken seriously as scholars in the field; and on the supposition that women may, at least sometimes, have a rather different perspective on questions about politics than men, it increases the probability that such different voices will be heard. This strategy can hold for courses in political philosophy, for example, whether those authors included do (Mary Wollstonecraft, Virginia Woolf's *Three Guineas*) or do not (Rosa Luxembourg, Hannah Arendt) discuss the situation of women from a feminist perspective in their work.

The injunction to cite women scholars because of the symbolic importance of seeing women's names in scholarly references holds good across the field. Some parts of the discipline have made more progress than others in articulating a feminist perspective, however, and women's issues in general are obviously more relevant to some topics than to others. It is hard to see how international relations or formal modelling have been much affected by scholarship on women; but in most other parts of the discipline—not only American government and political philosophy, but also comparative politics, political economy, public administration, and public law—it is possible to take a second step and include material that deals directly with the situation of women in political life. The tendency in many departments is to isolate such material in a single course on "Women in Politics." Such courses nourish and make use of scholarship on women. But it is at least equally important to integrate this material into other courses so that attention to women becomes a part of the study of "normal politics." A number of good review articles and bibliographies have recently appeared that make it easy for any concerned political scientist to take this step.[17]

A third step, which can be at least as instructive as the other two in quite a different way, is to notice passages in political science treatises from Aristotle to the most recent convention paper in which women are treated superficially, and gross or subtle prejudice takes the place of honest systematic inquiry. As soon as one becomes sensitive to such occurrences they leap out from numerous passages in some of the most prestigious literature in the field. One instance often cited by feminist critics is a section in Robert Lane's *Political Life* that argues against "politicizing the female role" on the grounds that "working girls and career women, . . . and women with extracurricular interests of an absorbing kind are often borrowing their time and attention and capacity for relaxed play and love from their children to whom it rightfully belongs," and are probably turning those offspring into juvenile delinquents and homosexuals.[18]

A host of fascinating questions about the ideology of differentiation, and the way it is perpetuated by scholarship, are raised by such assertions. A more elusive but equally interesting range of issues is raised when one takes a fourth step, and notices silences and absences. When discussions of "political man" are underway full throttle, we can stop and ask, "Does this author mean 'political woman,' too, or not? Did it ever occur to him to ask? If so, would he have been quite so ready to generalize about these aspects of political behavior?" As Ellen Boneparth puts it, "One of the most provocative questions one can ask is: 'Who is missing from this picture?' and 'Why?' The fact that women are not there is very much a social reality."[19]

Increasing numbers of teachers and researchers in political science, of both sexes, are using some combination of these four approaches to bring sensitivity to women's activities into their work. What difference has it made?

The early impact has been most noticeable in certain mainstream areas where new questions are appended to old agendas, without altering the way these questions are asked or answered in any very profound way. For instance, in studies of participation in America, survey researchers are now more attuned to the possibility that female respondents may differ, as voters, office-holders, and party activists, from their male counterparts, in interesting ways. The prominence of contemporary legal and moral issues involving women's rights—such as the ERA, equal opportunity, affirmative action, abortion and contraception—means that teaching and research in contemporary political philosophy and constitutional law are also more likely to address women's issues than was true in the recent past.

For political philosophers, such perennial issues as the definition of "equality," and what it means to say that someone's interests are "represented" by someone else, are illuminated by the concerns and achievements of the women's movement. "Equality as sameness" is clearly not a very attractive or plausible goal for most activists in the women's movement (or to their opponents either, for that matter); but how persons can be equal in important ways while differing on other significant dimensions of experience is a knotty and fascinating topic persistently presented by the movement for "equality between the sexes" in our time. Similar dilemmas are presented by the pressure to have women's interests represented in the political arena. How do we know whether there are any interests shared by all women? If there are, who speaks for them most persuasively: a strongly feminist female representative, a sympathetic male, or a women who rejects the "feminist" label but stands as living proof of the ambitions and competence of women? If one of the goals of the women's movement is to loosen the age-old tie between women and children in order to encourage everyone to think of women as persons first, rather than initially as mothers, and to present parenting as an occupation for both sexes, whose interests are served by focusing on issues such as child-care and maternity leave? Yet such interests are clearly of pressing importance for many women today, and if women in politics do not speak up for them, who will?

IV. Long-term implications

Such topics give political scientists new material to wrestle with, and novel evidence for their research, but do not alter the way questions are asked or evidence is gathered. Underneath such issues are more profound implications that could have a transforming effect upon the discipline itself. Thinking about several of these issues on the part of feminist scholars has proceeded far enough that we can see some of these implications already, though the discipline itself has hardly begun to notice them.[20]

One of the dichotomies political scientists take for granted is between "public" and "private" spheres of life. As we have seen, the "public" — or formal/legal — area of human life is normally associated with males, and the "private" — family and domestic life — especially with females. But these distinctions, for all their clear spatial associations "outside" and "inside" the home, are simply abstractions that ignore several of the most durable complexities in human life. By adopting these shorthand terms and relegating "private" life to some other discipline's concern, political science has begged many more questions than it has answered. Feminist scholarship is opening up this topic by demonstrating the selectively distorting effects of this ancient pigeonhole in our understanding of the world.[21]

On the one hand, feminists draw attention to patterns of authority within the family, traditionally dominated by the male head of house, which replicate in imagery and behavior some of the practices of the patriarchically-rooted polity. The importance of the family as an area for political education and the formation of opinions; as a key unit in the economy, which itself bridges domestic and political life; and as the locus for an impressive range of responsibilities and full-time demands (on women especially) that make mockery of the parallel associations of privacy with solitude and individuality: all these aspects of "private life" are now being brought to the fore, requiring us to rethink the old dichotomies. On the other hand, feminists point out the significance of informal male friendship networks in political life, and the attitude of powerful males towards females (secretaries and colleagues) as potential mistresses and body-servants or surrogate wives.

Feminists are also drawing attention to another aspect of human political life that effectively perpetuates male domi-nance: the close association of authority with the father. The cluster of connotations that brings together God, the *pater-familias*, and the head of state is very powerful and difficult to break apart. This ensures that any woman in a position of authority looks somehow odd and out of place. We have no good models for depicting women in authority, and the monopoly of the father-image is so complete that it is difficult to offer alternatives. The most obvious alternative—the maternal image—carries a very different set of connotations: of nurtur-ing, rather than commanding, of gentleness, not sternness. The general impropriety of adult males being subordinate to the rule of women carries over into a kind of contemptibility, as well; obedience to "mom" implies apronstrings and absence of manly maturity, far more than does deference to daddy.

Feminists trained in psychoanalysis are exploring the roots of such associations in the development of self-consciousness and awareness of the world in tiny infants. According to Dorothy Dinnerstein's provocative hypothesis, both men and women reject the authority of women because they associate it with the stage of full dependence on the mother, and the frustrations and intensities of the emotions associated with that period in our lives, whereas the authority of the father is comparatively imper-sonal and non-threatening to our identities.[22] Insofar as such insights are accurate we can understand how it is hard for us to accept the maternal image in the statehouse or White House. Other feminists are exploring different implications of the association of female authority with mothering: perhaps women do have different ways of conceptualizing and exercising power, by nature and experience, so that a world in which women hold authority would be more cooperative, more nurturant, less inclined to violence and braggadocio.[23] Perhaps on the other hand, testosterone is less important than situation, and women given power will behave very similarly to their male predecessors. Possibilities of both sorts are explored in various sectors of our contemporary consciousness (for example Gunter Grass's rich novel *The Flounder*); but they have yet to make much difference in the way the discipline of political science understands its central subject, the exercise of power.

Finally, a few radical feminists in America and a larger number of French writers are exploring the associations of language itself with male dominance and the perpetuation of a "phallogocentric" image of our world.[24] Such explorations move well beyond the obvious (though insufficiently appreciated) ways in which our languages support and reflect male supremacy—the so-called generic masculine, for example, or the practice of women taking on their husband's names. Beyond these, language in political life betrays the centrality of male experience in several subtle ways: in the use of metaphors such as "penetrate" and "thrust" in discussions of power-plays, and in the interchangeability of slang terms for describing sexual intercourse and aggressive taking-advantage-of another human being. In these linguistic facts, a male-centered understanding of the parallel experiences of aggressive sexuality and the exercise of political power is blatantly revealed. A female-centered language and literature would give more prominence to embracing, enfolding, blending, and sheltering, and so, supposedly, would a female-centered public life.

Anyone who makes this kind of effort at rethinking our language and the relationships between language patterns and the structures of social power engages in a bold and frustrating adventure, since language itself gives us our basic means of thinking through our world. Nonetheless, such exercises are germinal (no longer "seminal") in their implications for a science of human society and understanding all aspects of human life. Those of us who consider ourselves both feminists and political scientists have our work cut out for us. As Hegel put it long ago, *hic rhodus, hic salta,* which, loosely translated, means: there's plenty to do right here in reconstructing our discipline and eventually our public world.

NOTES

1. Mary L. Stanley and Victoria Schuck, "In Search of Political Woman," *Social Science Quarterly* LV: 3 (December 1974), p. 642: this essay forms part of a symposium on "Masculine Blinders in the Social Sciences." See also Susan C. Bourque and Jean Grossholtz, "Politics an Unnatural Practice: Political Science Looks at Female Participation," *Politics and Society* IV (Winter 1974), pp. 225–65; Wilma Rule Krauss, "Political Implications of Gender Roles: a Review of the Literature," *American Political Science Review* LXVIII (December 1974), pp. 1706–23; and only a few months later, Kay Boals, "Political Science," *Signs* I: 1 (Autumn 1975), pp. 161–74.
2. Jane Jaquette, ed., *Women in Politics* (New York: John Wiley), and Jeane Kirkpatrick, *Political Woman* (New York: Basic Books).
3. *American Politics Quarterly* V: 3 (July 1977); *Journal of Politics* XLI: 2 (May 1979); *Western Political Quarterly* and *American Political Science Review*, forthcoming.
4. Michelle Rosaldo, "The Use and Abuse of Anthropology: Reflections on Feminism and Cross-Cultural Understanding," *Signs* V: 3 (Spring 1980), 395. Sidney Verba, Norman Nie and Jae-On Kim, *Participation and Political Equality* (Cambridge University Press, 1978), report the same situation in their seven-nation sample (ch. 12).
5. Judith Evans, "Attitudes to Women in American Political Science," *Government & Opposition* XV: 1 (Winter 1980), p. 107, makes a similar point in an essay with an interesting critical perspective on the issue.
6. John Knox' *First Blast of the Trumpet Against the Monstrous Regiment of Women*, and Jean Bodin's speculations about the sexual favors of a female prince, are both discussed in Keohane, "Female Citizenship," a paper given at the Annual Meeting of the Conference for the Study of Political Thought in April 1979. In his comments on that paper Shlomo Avineri drew attention to the rich paradox that hierarchical societies are more likely to provide opportunities for women to hold high offices than those which profess more egalitarian ideologies.
7. William A. Hammond, "Women in Politics," *The North American Review* (1883), p. 144.
8. Rosabeth Moss Kanter, "Some Effects of Proportions on Group Life: Skewed Sex Ratios and Responses to Token Women," *American Journal of Sociology* LXXXII: 5 pp. 965–90, demonstrates that highly skewed ratios of two different human groups in a working situation puts special pressures on the members of the token minority.
9. Gianfranco Poggi, "The Place of Political Concerns in the Early Social Sciences," *Archives Européenes de Sociologie* XXI (1980), pp. 362–71, argues that the dominance of ancient formal traditions in the study of politics helped ensure that the nascent empirical social sciences "elected as privileged objects of their discourse the trite realities of everyday social practice." This division of scholarly labour must surely have paved the way for the earlier development of the study of women in these other disciplines.
10. *Politics*, book I (1260a); the word for "crown" here is *kosmon*, which means order, ornament, universe, good government, honor, decent behavior . . . and burial garment.
11. Emphasis added; I have seen this passage attributed to Carlyle, but have not been able to verify the location in his writings.

12. Robin Lakoff, *Language and Woman's Place* (New York: Harper & Row, 1975); Barrie Thorne and Nancy Henley, ed., *Language and Sex: Difference and Dominance* (Rowley, Mass.: Newbury House, 1975).
13. See, for example, *Émile*, book IV; in the Pléiade edition of Rousseau's *Oeuvres Complètes* (Paris: Gallimard, 1969), vol. IV, p. 518.
14. The Peloponnesian War, II: 7, in the Modern Library Edition of *The Complete Writings of Thucydides* (New York: Random House, 1951), p. 109.
15. *A New Look at the Silenced Majority: Women and American Democracy* (Englewood Cliffs, NJ: Prentice-Hall, 1977; first edition 1971).
16. Mary Lyndon Shanley, "Invisible Women: Thoughts on Teaching Political Philosophy," *News for Teachers of Political Science* (American Political Science Association publication), no. 24 (Winter 1980) pp. 2-4; Ellen Boneparth, "Integrating Materials on Women: American Government," *Ibid.*, no. 26 (Summer 1980), pp. 1-7.
17. In addition to works already cited, bibliographies of work about women and politics in various sub-fields are a regular feature of the journal *Women & Politics*. See also Karen Beckwith, "The Cross-Cultural Study of Women and Politics," in *Women & Politics* I: 2; Susan Moller Okin, *Women in Western Political Thought* (Princeton University Press 1979); Berenice Carroll, review essay "Political Science," *Signs* V: 2 and 3 (Winter 1979 and Spring 1980); and Cynthia Fuchs Epstein and Rose Laub Coser, eds., *Access to Power: Cross-National Studies of Women and Elites* (London: Allen & Unwin, 1981).
18. Robert Lane, *Political Life* (Glencoe, Free Press, 1959 and 1964), p. 355.
19. Ellen Boneparth, "Integrating Materials on Women," p. 1; Molly Shanley makes this same point by recalling Sherlock Holmes's story of the dog that *didn't* bark ("Invisible Women," p. 1).
20. Among the few pieces of work that combine conventional political science with ideas broached by radical feminist scholarship is William M. Lafferty, "Sex and Political Participation: an Exploratory Analysis of the 'Female Culture,'" *European Journal of Political Science* VIII: 3 (1980), pp. 323-47.
21. Scholars currently working in this area include Carole Pateman and Jane Flax, who have presented their findings in several provocative articles; see also Jean Bethke Elshtain's study of *Public Man, Private Woman* (Princeton University Press), and several essays in Zillah Eisenstein, ed., *Capitalist Patriarchy and the Case for Socialist Feminism* (New York and London: Monthly Review Press, 1979), and Michelle Rosaldo and Louise Lamphere, eds., *Woman, Culture and Society* (Stanford University Press, 1974).
22. *The Mermaid and the Minotaur: Sexual Arrangements and Human Malaise* (New York: Harper & Row, 1976). See also the work of Nancy Chodorow on *The Reproduction of Mothering* (University of California Press, 1978), a more scholarly and cautious statement of some parallel ideas.
23. Nancy Hartsock, *Money, Sex and Power* (forthcoming from Longman's) demonstrates that women writing about power—even women who are not feminists or especially concerned with women's issues, such as Hannah Arendt and Dorothy Emmett—offer descriptions of power that differ along these dimensions from those common to male political theorists.
24. Mary Daly, *Gyn/ecology* (Boston: Beacon Press, 1978) and Susan Griffin, *Woman and Nature* (New York: Harper & Row, 1978) are two prominent American examples; among French writers Hélène Cixous, Annie Leclerc, Luce Irigaray, Xavière Gauthier and Marguerite Duras are especially important.

HOW THE STUDY OF WOMEN HAS RESTRUCTURED THE DISCIPLINE OF ECONOMICS

NANCY S. BARRETT

I N REFLECTING ON THE SIGNIFICANCE of women's studies for the traditional assumptions of the discipline of economics, this paper will refer primarily to the mainstream, or "neoclassical," school of economics. This is not to say that the study of women has not had its effects on other branches as well—most notably the Marxian school. However, exploring the impacts on neoclassical thinking is suggestive of the influence that women's studies have had on the range of paradigms that constitute the discipline of economics.

The assumption of individualism and individual self-determination is essential to neoclassical economic thought. Neoclassical analysis is derived from the laissez-faire doctrine of nineteenth-century liberalism that viewed individual choices made in a competitive, free-enterprise marketplace as the means of achieving the highest level of material well-being for society as a whole.[1] In economic jargon, laissez-faire, competition, and individual choice produce "efficient" resource allocation. The "invisible hand" doctrine, on which neoclassical analysis is based, has as its underlying proposition that if individuals and competitive firms are left to seek their own private gain, the "invisible hand" of the market will guide them to the most advantageous choices, and thereby the material welfare of society will be

Nancy S. Barrett is a Professor of Economics at American University in Washington, D.C. She is the author of several books including, *Prices and Wages in U.S. Manufacturing*, and *The Theory of Macroeconomic Policy*. She has written numerous articles on economic policy, labor markets, and related issues and was a major contributor to *The Subtle Revolution*, a collection of works on the growth of the female labor force. She received her Ph.D. in economics from Harvard University.

maximized. Thus, unfettered individualism was believed to result in social harmony and the highest level of material well-being. This conclusion provided a moral justification to free-enterprise capitalism which underlies the positivistic or "scientifically objective" framework of neoclassical thinking.

I. The Impetus for Studying Women's Economic Status

Given the individualistic bent of mainstream economic analysis and the positivistic approach characteristic of much of contemporary social science methodology, it is not surprising that economists traditionally were not interested in studying women as a separate group—at least until the mid-1960s. There had been a few exceptions—notably in economic history and a few scattered studies of household technology. But, in fact, most workers were assumed to be men, whose only time-use options were "work" (paid employment) and "leisure." Consumers on the other hand were generally assumed to live in (family) units with common "utility functions." But starting in the mid-1960s a new body of research on discrimination and labor market segmentation began to develop.[2] The Civil Rights Act of 1964, and the passage of a whole series of laws and executive orders regarding equal employment opportunity, opened up the question of discrimination in labor markets as a major policy issue. In order to implement this legislation, it was necessary to establish whether in fact discrimination in labor markets was actually occurring, or rather whether existing wage differentials by race and sex could be attributed to factors other than discrimination. Since economists were presumably the keepers of the discipline that analyzed labor market behavior, they were called in to provide assistance for resolving this important policy question. This, quite naturally, led economists to explore the question of women's relatively inferior economic status.[3]

II. Individualism Versus Sexism

Before considering how economists actually addressed the problem, it will be instructive to think in the abstract about how gender (sex) might, in and of itself, impinge upon resource allocation in a neoclassical view of the economy. That is, to what extent do the personal characteristics of individuals (in this case sex) make a difference in the allocative process?

Personal characteristics become significant only to the extent that they affect economic choices or preferences, on the one hand, and economic contributions, or productivity, on the other. Thus, on the product-market side, women may prefer different types of consumption goods from men (due either to their genetic makeup or to social conditioning), and these preferences affect their market behavior. However, what is of primary interest for studies of discrimination is why labor market outcomes differ by sex. These could be due either to sex-related preferences—in this case for certain types of jobs or training opportunities—on the one hand, or to differences in ability that affect worker productivity on the other.

Thus, it is perfectly consistent with the neoclassical view of labor markets for women (as a group) to be earning less than men (as a group) if women are inherently less productive than men, or if they prefer to acquire less education and training, or if they prefer lower-paying jobs that require less effort and responsibility than those that men prefer. From an economist's point of view, it does not matter whether these differences in tastes are innate or developed through social conditioning. Only when equally qualified men and women with identical tastes fail to attain equal job status would neoclassical analysis attribute the outcome to a failure of markets or "discrimination."[4]

Concern with the relatively inferior economic status of women—women, on average, earn about 60 percent of the male wage, even when they work full time—led to the development of labor market theories that attempted to explain sex differences in economic success. Initially, this literature focused on the issue of whether women's inferior position was somehow justified, that is, whether it was the result of freely-made choices of women themselves or of women's lesser inherent ability, rather than of discrimination against women by someone else. Eventually, however, the analysis called into question the fundamental validity of the neoclassical assumption of efficient markets, and with it the ethical or moral rationale for free enterprise capitalism itself.

Again, concentrating on the mainstream component of the discipline of economics, two basic approaches emerged. One of these, the *human capital school,* was essentially an extension of the neoclassical approach to labor markets. The second, what I will call the *institutionalist school,* called into question many of the basic premises of the neoclassical approach.

III. Human Capital Theory

The human capital explanation of sex-based differences in economic success is an attempt to establish the extent to which labor market outcomes are "explainable" on the basis of tastes and productivity-related characteristics (human capital).[5] In this context, a wage differential between men and women is totally consistent with the neoclassical theory of labor markets, provided that these relationships can be established. Wage differentials between men and women, according to this view, are due to differences in human capital, to preferences for certain types of jobs, and in some cases to preferences on the parts of employers and co-workers for "discriminating" against women.

One difficulty with establishing the validity of this approach is that the concept of human capital is highly subjective. In fact, some proponents would argue tautologically that human capital is whatever enables a worker to earn more than some other worker. Proxies for human capital include education and work experience. However, most studies of male and female workers having the same amounts of education and work experience still find very large, unexplained differences between male and female earnings.[6] That is, measured human capital variables explain very little of the male-female earnings gap. Measuring the extent to which preferences for lesser-paid work influence wage differentials is virtually impossible, as it is impossible to obtain any quantitative measure of preferences.

If one is to hold to the neoclassical view (1) that individuals shape institutions, and (2) that individual characteristics are significant only as they affect consumption patterns or productivity, that is, if one is to hold on to the purely positivistic approach to economic analysis, the empirical task is to uncover ever more "relevant" characteristics to "explain" the differences between male and female earnings and other differences in economic outcomes. From a "theoretical" point of view, one can simply assert that men and women acquire different amounts of human capital, that their human capital differs in quality, or that their preferences are different — due either to innate differences between the sexes or differences in the way that the sexes are socialized. In fact, if the basic postulates of neoclassical economic theory — profit maximization, efficient markets, etc. — are to remain intact, some form of human capital explanation of wage differentials must be proved valid. No wonder, then, that the mainstream of the economics profession clings so tenaciously to human capital explanations and seeks diligently for more comprehensive measures to account for the wage gap between men and women.

IV. The Institutionalist Approach

Skeptics of the human capital approach have turned to other explanations of women's inferior economic status. These explanations call into question the basic positivistic premises of the neoclassical analysis. Perhaps the most basic proposition called into question is that relative wages are market-determined. According to what has been called the "institutionalist" view, the relative wages of men and women are less the outcomes of supply and demand interactions than a mirror of the relative positions of men and women in society.[7] That is, to the extent that society assigns a lesser value to women's work, to the extent that it is widely believed that women's subsistence needs are less than men's, or that women don't "need" high paying jobs, women will be paid less than men.[8] Taking the analysis one step further, one could argue that the wage structure itself has been a major (if not *the* major) factor perpetuating sex-based status differences in society.

During the industrial revolution in nineteenth-century England, there were many more workers available than jobs in industry and, hence, workers had practically no bargaining power. With a virtually infinite supply of labor, wages could theoretically be driven to near zero; however, the perceived subsistence requirements of workers are a factor. Contemporary records show that women's wages were set at around 60 percent of men's, purportedly because of women's lower subsistence requirements. Because single women workers' subsistence needs were presumed to be less than the needs of men with families to support, and married women were assumed to be merely supplementing their husbands' income, employers felt justified in paying women less. Moreover, equal pay would have been inconsistent with the established order of male dominance.[9] However, as labor market rewards increasingly determined an individual's status, lower pay scales for women were at once a cause and effect of women's inferior social position.[10]

It must be understood that this institutionalist view of women's earnings has very radical implications for neoclassical economics. In the conventional neoclassical paradigm, human beings are viewed as inputs into the production process very much like capital equipment and raw materials. As consumers, human beings are viewed by neoclassical economics as inherently hedonistic, the goal of their activities being to maximize their psychic gratification from goods and services. But as workers, individuals are assumed to be totally unaware of the psychic aspects of the work environment.[11] It is inherently very difficult to imagine that human beings can relate to each other as "pleasure machines" in one context, and yet to ignore basic social interactions in the workplace.

If sociology is to be a consideration in the analysis of labor market behavior, then surely sex differences in job assignments and in the valuation of work must emerge. Across no other characteristic is a socioeconomic status differential so deeply engrained as across sexes. In every society in recorded history, including the most primitive societies, there has been a status differential based on sex. Moreover, in every known society, there has been an economic division of labor based on sex. In no society have men and women been assigned the same economic roles, and in no society has the status of women's work been the same as the status of men's work.

The reason that the institutionalist view has such radical implications for neoclassical economic thought is that it raises questions concerning the entire theory of wage determination, of the efficiency of free markets and of capitalist institutions, and of the equity of an income distribution based upon the Horatio Alger ideal. That is, it raises fundamental questions concerning the inherent justice of wage outcomes in a freely functioning competitive market. If rewards are based on sociological considerations rather than on the skill and effort that is put into work, then it is not altogether clear that the traditional justification for free-enterprise capitalism remains.

The institutionalist approach also raises questions about the traditional remedies for inequality and discrimination. According to the human capital approach, inequality can be remedied through providing better access to human capital for all. This means eliminating discrimination in education and providing women and other disadvantaged persons with more work experience and better-quality work experience, as well as changing personal "preferences" for sex-segregated occupational assignments. According to the institutional view, however, it is impossible to legislate equality. Instead, what is needed is a complete societal revolution in sex roles. Unless this happens, it is impossible to achieve equality simply by giving everyone equal access.

V. Implications

The insights gleaned from the study of women in the work force have extremely profound consequences not only for the allocative implications of laissez-faire market capitalism but also for some of its presumed moral attributes—raising questions of justice and the ethical content of freedom. They also call into question the notion that economic status determines social status. Rather, economic status may well be a reflection of societal worth or status judgments.

Another implication is that economics holds out no solution to the enigma of why women continue to be judged inferior to men in all aspects of life. Women are not second-class citizens because they are less productive or because they prefer lower-paying jobs. They are economically discriminated against because society does not value women's worth as highly as that of men.

Women's studies should continue to be an interdisciplinary activity, precisely because the study of women through the perspective of any one discipline is likely to lead squarely into another. What the interdisciplinary approach should explore is the root of these social judgments of the worth of women. Anthropology, sociology, economics, and psychology all seem to leave as a fundamental mystery the root of the problem of women's inferior status. This is not to say that economic remedies are not a powerful antidote to discrimination against women in the labor market, and should not be used much more aggressively than they have been to date. But economic science, as a discipline, has very little to offer in terms of explaining the fundamental reason why a sex-based status differential has been so deeply engrained in all societies. Full economic equality for women cannot be achieved until this question has been answered and the problem resolved at its most basic level.

NOTES

1. This proposition was articulated and first popularized in Adam Smith, *The Wealth of Nations*, 1776. A recent rearticulation is in Milton Friedman, *Capitalism and Freedom* (Chicago: University of Chicago Press, 1962).
2. See, for instance, Peter B. Doeringer and Michael J. Piore, *Internal Labor Markets and Manpower Analysis* (Heath, 1971); Michael Reich, David M. Gordon and Richard C. Edwards, "A Theory of Labor Market Segmentation," *American Economic Review*, (May, 1973); Barbara Bergmann, "The Effect on White Incomes of Discrimination in Employment," *Journal of Political Economy* (March/April, 1971); Victor Fuchs, "Differences in Hourly Earnings between Men and Women," *Monthly Labor Review* (May, 1971); Orley Ashenfelter and Albert Rees, *Discrimination in Labor Markets* (Princeton University Press, 1973).
3. Economists had, of course, analyzed wage differentials prior to their interest in sex-related wage differences. These differentials were examined, in part, because they were associated with "immobilities" between labor markets separated by space, skill requirements, etc. Sex differences also involve immobility, but the issue here is why sex, in and of itself, should have any relevance to wages—that is, why should there be different labor markets for men and women?
4. Even in this case, neoclassical analysis could attribute the differential to a "taste for discrimination" on the part of employers or co-workers. See Gary S. Becker, *The Economics of Discrimination* (Chicago: University of Chicago Press, 1957).
5. Examples of the human capital literature include: G. S. Becker, "Investment in Human Capital: A Theoretical Analysis", *Journal of Political Economy*, Special Supplement (October, 1962), sect. 2; Jacob Mincer, *Labor Force Participation of Married Women: A Study of Labor Supply*, in National Bureau of Economic Research, *Aspects of Labor Economics* (Princeton: Princeton University Press, 1962), pp. 63–97; Glen G. Cain, *Married Women in the Labor Force* (Chicago: The University of Chicago Press, 1966); T. W. Schultz, "Investment in Human Capital", *American Economic Review*, (March, 1961); Jacob Mincer and Solomon Polachek, "Family Investments in Human Capital: Earnings of Women," *Journal of Political Economy*, (March/April, 1974).
6. See, for instance, Isabel V. Sawhill, "The Economics of Discrimination Against Women: Some New Findings," *Journal of Human Resources*, (Summer, 1973); and Alan S. Blinder, "Wage Discrimination: Reduced Form and Structural Estimates," *Journal of Human Resources*, (Fall, 1973).
7. See, for instance, Barbara Bergmann, "Reducing the Pervasiveness of Discrimination," in Eli Ginzburg (ed.) *Jobs for Americans* (Prentice-Hall, 1976); Alice H. Amsden, *The Economics of Women and Work* (Penguin Books, Reading in Economics Series), 1979; and Nancy S. Barrett, "Women in the Job Market," in Ralph Smith (ed.), *The Subtle Revolution* (The Urban Institute, 1979).
8. There is even a Biblical reference to segregated pay scales. Leviticus (27:1-4) describes a conversation between the Lord and Moses in which adult males are valued at 50 shekels of silver and adult females at 30 shekels—a ratio strongly like that encountered today. Possibly the different pay rates for men and women in primitive society were linked to their relative ability to perform hard manual labor—a rationale that today's advance technology has made obsolete.

9. For a revealing account of employment and pay practices and attitudes toward women workers during this period see Ivy Pinchbeck, *Women Workers in the Industrial Revolution* (London: G. Routledge, 1930).

10. The tendency of the industrial wage structure to reproduce preindustrial status hierarchies rather than to reflect the relative skill or productivity of classes of workers was noted by John Stuart Mill in 1848. See J.S. Mill, *Principles of Political Economy*, Vol. 2.

11. Some writers have noted the "psychic" rewards from work as being a part of an individual's income. However, if psychic rewards are a part of income, disagreeable jobs should pay more than other jobs. In fact, workers who perform heavy, dirty, tedious, or otherwise distasteful work usually earn less than workers in cleaner, easier, and more interesting jobs. Moreover, if psychic rewards are higher in jobs requiring more skill, it would seem that wage differentials should be less than training costs. In fact, empirical evidence suggests that the reverse is the case, that the more training is required the greater the differential that cannot be attributed to the training costs.

ANTHROPOLOGY AND
THE STUDY OF GENDER

JUDITH SHAPIRO

THIS PAPER WAS PREPARED for a lecture series entitled "Studying Women: The Impact on the Social Sciences and Humanities." I might have followed the general theme of the series by calling my own paper "Anthropology and the Study of Women." I felt it important, however, to define my subject as the study of gender rather than the study of women. Let me begin by discussing why I considered this reformulation necessary.

The anthropological studies of sex roles that have appeared in recent years have been primarily studies of women. This is not surprising, since the resurgence of feminism in the 1960s led to a growing interest in the question of gender in various academic fields.[1] There are problems, however, in defining our enterprise as the study of women, and the first I would like to point out is what can be called the problem of *markedness*. I borrow this term from linguists and semioticians, who use it to refer to an asymmetrical relationship between a pair of categories that constitute complementary opposites within some larger class.[2] The terms "man" and "woman," for example, serve to contrast male and female members of the larger class of human beings; as such, they appear to be complementary opposites. At the same time, the term "man," as we know, can be used in a more general sense to contrast the human species as a whole with some other category. Thus, the terms "man" and "woman" designate

Judith Shapiro is an Associate Professor of Anthropology at Bryn Mawr College. She has carried out field research with two tribal societies in Brazil, the Tapirapé and Yanomama, and has also worked with the Northern Paiute of Nevada. Her publications have been primarily in the areas of social organization, kinship, and sex roles. She is currently engaged in the study of missionaries.

110

categories that are also in a hierarchical relationship, since one of the terms can be used to refer to the wider class as a whole, in effect subsuming what is its opposite term at a lower level of contrast. In oppositions of this sort, the more general term is referred to as the "unmarked" member of the pair, while the other, more restricted in its meaning, is the "marked" term. Feminists have themselves called attention to the asymmetry of gender categories in language, which operates in pronouns as well. The use of the pronoun "his" in the phrase "everyone should weed his own garden" is appropriate whether the suggestion is being made to an all-male group or a mixed one. The phrase "everyone should weed her own garden," however, restricts the class of appropriate subjects to female.

The relatively unmarked quality of maleness, reflected in the tendency to equate masculinity with humanity in general, has also been documented in the field of psychology. A well-known and often-cited study by Inge Broverman and her colleagues reported that psychologists' profiles of the mentally healthy person (when sex was not specified) corresponded to profiles of the healthy man. Profiles of the healthy or normal woman were different and included qualities—for example, dependency, emotionality, excitability—that were not considered signs of good mental health in a general, sexually unmarked context (Broverman et al. 1970).

Feminist scholars from a variety of different fields have pointed to how their respective disciplines have presented a male-oriented perspective on the human condition. The emergence of women's studies programs is thus a reflection of the extent to which the apparently unmarked courses in the academic curriculum constitute a *de facto* men's studies program. By teaching courses on women, focusing our research efforts on women, we bring those who have been in the darkness out into the light.

Anthropologists engaged in women's studies often note that their approach is not merely additive, but rather calls for a basic rethinking of the relationship between the sexes. Their immediate contributions, however, have tended to be concerned fairly exclusively with women. This may have been a fruitful short-term strategy, but in the long run could become self-defeating, since it perpetuates the marked status of women. We have, on the one side, women's studies and, on the other, the traditional fields of study, to varying degrees male-oriented but still ostensibly unmarked. Women are seen as a problem requiring some kind of special attention, while men are more or less taken for granted, or at least not focused upon in a comparably explicit way. But would it not be better to view men as being just as problematic as women? To insist that we need more studies of men *as men* — that is, studies based not on an uncritical assumption that what men do is more interesting or important than what women do, but studies carried out with a particular focus on gender?

Another problem with saying we are "studying women," aside from the issue of markedness, is that this phrasing seems to designate a class of individual objects rather than an analytic category. It is important to stress that our subject is not "women" (or, for that matter, "men") as groups of individuals, but rather gender as an aspect of social identity. We should be careful not to imply that identity is coterminous with gender.

In treating women as a group or category apart, we fail to pose a sufficiently pointed challenge to the traditional fields of scholarly inquiry. The charge that women have been relatively ignored by the social sciences, while true, does not adequately address the problem. The real issue, in my opinion, is that the social sciences have yet to come to terms with gender as a social fact. They have suffered from a tendency to relegate sex to the domain of the infra-social, to view sex roles largely in terms of how biology constrains society.[3] The message from current sex-role research is that gender must be viewed from the perspectives of economics, politics, religion, philosophy, art — in brief, that gender is a total social fact that takes on its meaning and function from the wider cultural system of which it is a part.

The task before us, as I see it, is one of making it as impossible for social scientists to avoid dealing with gender in their studies of social differentiation as it is for them to avoid dealing with such things as rank, class, and kinship. The goal is to integrate the study of gender differences into the central pursuits of the social sciences and, in turn, to see in what way these pursuits are modified and refined by understanding the particular features of gender as a principle of social organization. I do not know whether this is the impact that recent studies of women have as yet had on the social sciences generally, or on anthropology in particular, but I maintain that it is the impact that they can have and should have.

Before considering the relationship between sex-role studies and the wider field of anthropology, I should say something about how I am using the terms "sex" and "gender." While these terms can mean a number of different things, I have found that they serve a particularly useful analytic purpose in contrasting a set of biological facts with a set of cultural facts. Were I to be scrupulous in my use of terms, I would use the term "sex" only when I was speaking of biological differences between males and females, and use "gender" whenever I was referring to the social, cultural, psychological constructs that are imposed upon these biological differences. The meaning of the term "gender," as I understand it, is thus not unlike its meaning for grammarians: it designates a set of categories to which we can give the same label cross-linguistically, or cross-culturally, because they have some connection to sex differences. These categories are, however, conventional or arbitrary insofar as they are not reducible to or directly derivative of natural, biological facts; they vary from one language to another, one culture to another, in the way in which they order experience and action.

The reader may notice that I have several times used the term "sex" when "gender" would have been the analytically appropriate choice. In doing this, I have bowed to common patterns of usage. I do not think this poses a serious problem, since context should make it clear whether I am speaking of biology or culture. The terminological opposition between sex and gender remains available for times when I want to draw an explicit contrast between biological differences and cultural patterns, and I make use of it for that purpose.

Let me now go on to discuss how gender studies fit within certain more general trends in anthropology and consider some of the theoretical issues they have raised. I will not be attempting any general survey of the literature.[4] I will limit myself to outlining a few major themes, drawing on selected studies for purposes of illustration. The themes I will be developing are the following: (1) how the study of gender fits within what has come to be known as symbolic anthropology; (2) how the study of gender has raised new theoretical problems for the understanding of social hierarchy, or inequality; and (3) how the study of gender brings to the fore issues concerning the sociology of knowledge, a central concern of all social scientists.

I. Gender and Symbol

Over the last couple of decades, there has been a movement within anthropology to focus particular attention on the symbolic dimension of human social life. Some of the major contributors to this orientation include such British anthropologists as Victor Turner, Edmund Leach, Rodney Needham, and Mary Douglas; in America, the major figures associated with this approach include Clifford Geertz and David Schneider. The theoretical orientation they represent has come to be known as symbolic anthropology, or cultural analysis. Actually, insofar as "culture," the master concept of anthropology, is defined in terms of the symbolic nature of human behavior, one might imagine that all of anthropology is symbolic anthropology. However, not all approaches in anthropology give equal emphasis to the symbolic function. Indeed, many theories in effect fail to take account of it at all. Symbolic anthropologists define themselves in opposition to those who view human behavior within naturalist, materialist or utilitarian perspectives. Symbolic anthropology has thus emerged as a theoretical alternative to such approaches in anthropology as cultural ecology (in which emphasis is given to the human group's need to adapt to its natural environment); cultural materialism (which combines technological/environmental determinism with an attempt to account for human social institutions in practical, utilitarian terms); and transactional, game theory orientations (in which the focus is on the maximizing individual — another kind of utilitarian approach). Central to symbiotic anthropology is the concept of the arbitrariness of the symbol. Cultures, like languages or literary texts, are meaningful systems; the goal when one approaches them is less explanation, as one understands this in the tradition of the natural sciences, than it is interpretation.

Studies of gender carried out within the framework of symbolic anthropology have helped us to realize that the meaning of male and female is neither self-evident nor everywhere the same. They have contributed toward the conceptualization of gender, discussed above, as an arbitrary or conventional system. Some of the best such work has come out of recent ethnographic studies in Melanesia. As long ago as Gregory Bateson's classic study of the *naven* ceremony among the Iatmul of New Guinea (Bateson [1936] 1958), this part of the world has proven a particularly rich area for the study of beliefs about gender and the stylization of feminine and masculine behavior. Research carried out in recent years has deepened our understanding of beliefs about gender and sexuality, and shown how these beliefs must be understood within their wider cultural contexts. I will cite just a few studies to serve as examples.

In research carried out among the Etoro of highland New Guinea, Raymond Kelly has explored the cultural connections between sexuality, witchcraft, and beliefs about the nature of men and women (Kelly 1976). According to Kelly, the domains of witchcraft and sexual relations are ordered by a common set of concepts and should thus be studied together for the light they shed on one another. Both must be understood with reference to Etoro concepts of life-force, which may be increased or diminished, and the importance of semen as a vital substance determining the degree of a man's life-force. A man acquires semen in his early years and loses it in the course of his lifetime, both through acts of heterosexual intercourse and through serving as a donor to a younger male whose growth he thereby insures. The oral-genital transfer of semen links men together in a chain of being, through a closed energy system in which the younger literally feed upon the older and are nurtured at their expense. Heterosexual activity is associated with death and depletion for the man; the woman, for her part, serves as an agent of depletion without herself benefiting from the transfer of male substance. Because of the dangers heterosexual intercourse poses for the man, it is cause for considerable ambivalence and is hedged by many restrictions. These negative attitudes do not apply to homosexual activity; while such activity has a tragic dimension for the older partner, it is regarded as a necessary part of maturation and is viewed in a generally positive light.

In the Etoro social universe, witches, who may be either male or female, are those who prey upon the souls, or spirit doubles, of others and consume a portion of their victims' life-force in this manner. Witchcraft and sexual relations thus pose similar threats to a man's vital substance, and women can be compared to witches, who are depletors *par excellence,* the embodiment of all that is antisocial and therefore evil. Moreover, if there is a metaphorical relationship between witches and women in general, the woman who tempts her husband into excessive sexual activity is likely to be seen as a true witch.

In the Etoro case, then, one achieves a richer understanding of gender and sexuality through taking account of such other aspects of culture as witchcraft beliefs. These domains interpenetrate, provide idioms for one another. It is important to see that the relationship works both ways: if gender and sexuality can serve as metaphors for other areas of life, so gender and sexuality take on their own meaning from other domains of experience. If we turn to our own society, we can see that the oppositions we draw between masculinity and femininity and the sense we make of sexual activity can only be understood with reference to a variety of cultural notions, of which competition, achievement, rationality, irrationality, love, and nature are but a few. The study of gender concepts, sex roles, and female-male relations thus becomes part of a more general symbolic analysis.

Kelly's account of the Etoro, it should be pointed out, presents the male perspective. This observation is not intended as a criticism of Kelly, who is an outstanding ethnographer and recognizes this limitation himself; in his view, it would have been impossible for a male researcher to work closely with Etoro women (Kelly 1976:47). What we must keep in mind is that we do not know which of the beliefs outlined by Kelly are generally shared by all Etoro and which are peculiar to the men. If women have a different set of beliefs, different perspectives on such matters as witchcraft and sexuality, these remain to be discovered and interpreted. The general question of the divergence between men's and women's world views, and the related issue of how the sex of the researcher may affect the outcome of the research, will be treated in a later section of this paper. For now, though, I would like to mention another symbolic analysis of gender which, as it happens, was produced by a woman anthropologist who was explicitly concerned with supplementing and correcting the account of a particular society that had been produced earlier by a male ethnographer.

There are certain societies that are part of the common culture of all anthropologists, since they have been the subject of a classic ethnography or set of ethnographies. One such case is that of the Trobriand Islanders, whose way of life was described in the various writings of Bronislaw Malinowski. Among the anthropologists who have studied the Trobrianders more recently, one, Annette Weiner, came to focus her attention on Trobriand women, since she felt that Malinowski had failed to accord sufficient importance to women in his own accounts; notably, he had failed to appreciate the social and symbolic significance of women's role in the system of exchanges that occupies a central place in Trobriand life. Weiner's reanalyses of Trobriand society (Weiner 1976, 1979, 1980) emphasize the symbolic dimension of exchange; they provide interpretations of the exchange activities of men and women in terms of Trobriand cosmological beliefs about complementary roles of women and men in the reproduction of life, and in the development and replacement of social persons. Charging that social anthropologists have commonly taken too narrow a view of the social order, Weiner expands the scope of her analysis to include the cosmic order, providing new perspectives on Trobriand matriliny and the "power" of women.

Weiner's goals in analyzing Trobriand sex roles and gender concepts go beyond the interpretation of a particular society. She uses the Trobriand case as a basis for broad cross-cultural generalization about gender symbolism and the respective value different societies place on maleness and femaleness (Weiner 1976: 233-6). The Trobrianders become a prototypical case of all those societies that differ from us in their ability to recognize and accord proper value to certain presumably inherent qualities of womanhood.[5] We see here a convergence of the world view of the Trobrianders and the ideological concerns of the researcher (assuming that the ethnography is itself only minimally the anthropologist's own projection, a point we must keep in mind when approaching any ethnographic account). Trobriand woman, in standing for all that our own male-oriented culture denies, serves to "balance the books," to present an alternative reality in which women are seen as important and exercise significant kinds of power. She is a foil much as the Noble Savage was for philosophers commenting on European society from the sixteenth century onward.

It is interesting to compare Weiner's work with another symbolic analysis of gender that also occupies an important place in the emerging body of anthropological literature on women. Sherry Ortner has written an article based on the question of whether male is to female as culture is to nature (Ortner 1974). Developing one of the major themes in the work of the French anthropologist Claude Lévi-Strauss, Ortner suggests that there is such a parallel. She gives biological reasons for why the equations between women and nature/men and culture might emerge as cross-cultural universals, but ultimately locates the equations and the asymmetry between them in the realm of ideology. She accounts for what she sees as a universal subordination of women to men by the universal social valuation of culture over nature. Ortner's argument has provoked much debate. One major question is whether the conceptual opposition she draws between nature and culture, and the hierarchical relationship between them, represent valid cross-cultural generalizations or are rather representations of our own culture's system of ideas.[6]

The basic impulse of symbolic anthropology has been toward the achievement of rich descriptions and interpretations of particular other cultures. Anthropologists working under this rubric have called into question traditional comparative frameworks that depend on pulling items of a cultural repertoire out of their contexts, and on coding as similar practices that may look alike but mean different things. There are some symbolic anthropologists, like Weiner and Ortner, who have sought to move beyond analyzing the symbol systems of individual cultures; here, the movement has been a direct leap into broad generalizations. The coming years will perhaps see progress toward achieving comparisons that are more detailed, close-grained, and revealing of the specific similarities and differences between the conceptualizations of gender found in various cultural settings. If the field of gender studies moves in this direction, it will be in a position to contribute to the elaboration of comparative strategies in symbolic anthropology more generally. In any event, it is clear that symbolic analyses of gender will continue to constitute a particularly fertile field for anthropological research and writing.[7]

II. Gender and Social Hierarchy

Given the feminist context of recent anthropological research on sex roles and women, a central preoccupation in the literature has been the issue of sexual inequality. How should it be described and analyzed? What are its causes? Is it universal? Is it inevitable?

My own doctoral research among the Yanomama Indians of northern Brazil dealt with the issue of sexual hierarchy, a topic I came to while doing field research during the late 60s. I tried to explore how we could characterize the asymmetry between men's and women's positions in society. I discussed differences in work patterns and social networks, contrasts in the degree of structural elaboration and formalization of men's and women's social roles, differential access of men and women to public statuses and valued sacred knowledge, and the control by men of the marriage system (Shapiro 1972, 1976). The attempt to arrive at a cross-cultural formulation of sexual inequality was also a major goal of what has been perhaps the most influential single publication in the anthropological field of women's studies, a volume of essays entitled *Woman, Culture, and Society* (Rosaldo and Lamphere 1974). Ortner's article appeared in this collection, complementing other contributions that analyzed the opposition between "domestic" and "public" domains and considered the effects of women's child-rearing role (Rosaldo 1974, Chodorow 1974).

Ortner's and Weiner's respective symbolic analyses of gender, outlined in the previous section, reflect this central concern with sexual inequality and illustrate the bipolar response of feminist scholars. One response is to affirm the universality of male dominance and to seek ways of accounting for it without falling into biological determinism. Another is to deny the generality of the pattern by producing cases to serve as counterexamples; anthropologists taking this position are concerned with showing how sexual differentiation may imply complementarity as well as inequality.

A number of anthropologists have attempted to explain cross-cultural differences and similarities in the positions of the sexes by means of one kind of economic theory or another. One attempt at a general comparison is a study by Ernestine Friedl (1975), which presents an overview of sex roles in foraging and horticultural societies. Friedl tries to account for the relative power of men and women in terms of who controls production and extra-domestic exchange. She explores reasons why men are generally more likely than women to obtain such control, but also tries to identify reasons for variation.[8]

Other economic approaches to the relative status of men and women have been more sharply focused around Marxist concepts. Marxist analyses can take essentially two forms. One is to approach the sexes themselves as if they were classes, and describe the relations between them in essentially the same language as one might use to analyze the relationship between proletariat and bourgeoisie. Concepts used to discuss control over the means of production are applied to the means of biological and social reproduction as well; patrilineal descent systems, for example, may be viewed in the light of how senior males appropriate the fruits of women's labor in reproduction and socialization (O'Laughlin 1974).

Another kind of Marxist approach lies in seeing the development of sexual inequality as a function of the emergence of class systems. Such studies have contributed importantly to an understanding of the significance of gender roles for the operation of class systems. As Leacock (1975) has pointed out, we must not think of women and the domestic realm as belonging to some separate sphere irrelevant for the economist analyzing capitalist society; on the contrary, particular patterns of gender roles and family organization are an intrinsic part of how this type of society operates.

The general attempt to explain sexual stratification by class stratification is, however, unsatisfactory; it simply flies in the face of too much ethnographic data. Such data are sometimes dismissed by Marxist scholars, who claim that accounts of sexual hierarchy in tribal societies are artifacts of colonial rule rather than accurate representations of aboriginal institutions. Anthropologists have, to be sure, generally been remiss in observing how the colonial context and history of contact have affected the subjects of their studies. There is, moreover, ample evidence of cases in which women's status declined sharply under colonial regimes; documenting this process has, in fact, been an important contribution of anthropologists and other social scientists working in the so-called Third World.[9] It is clear, however, that the ethnographic record does not support an attempt to blame male dominance on capitalism or to see sexual inequality as a legacy of colonialism. Nor can all "aboriginal" cases of sexual differentiation be read as involving complementarity rather than hierarchy, unless we are prepared to read our own case in those terms as well.

Marxist idealizations of sex-role differentiation in small-scale societies bring us back to the Noble Savage; what we are seeing is an attempt to seek a charter for social change in the myth of a Golden Age. This approach is also a way of avoiding one of the thornier problems that recent sex-role studies have raised for the field of anthropology, which is the question of whether and how we can go about adopting a critical perspective on societies very different from our own. The union between social science and social criticism is one thing when we are questioning our own institutions, moving in our own moral universe. If we engage in a critique of other cultures, however, do we risk engaging in what we have generally seen as the opposite of anthropology—missionization? Then there is the danger that lies in the other direction. In terms of social science theory, the alternatives to critical approaches—which emphasize such issues as conflict, inequality, exploitation, and contradiction—are theoretical orientations that at the least do not question and at the most positively celebrate things as they are. Do we operate with a theoretical double standard: a critique of society for us and functionalism for the natives?

The way out of these difficulties lies in the development of an appropriate comparative framework for dealing with social hierarchy. Gender studies should play a central role in this development, for which they have already provided an impetus. It has become clear from anthropological studies of sex roles carried out thus far that attempts to make cross-cultural comparisons about the "status" of women *per se* are problematic. Criteria appear to be either ethnocentric or governed by a misguided concept of objectivity, or both. There is also a growing realization on the part of some anthropologists that the status of women, or even the respective positions of women and men, cannot be approached as a self-contained issue. The study of gender ranking must be part of a more general inquiry into social hierarchy; patterns of gender asymmetry in a particular society are to be understood in the context of whatever other patterns of social inequality obtain in that society.[10] Indeed, one way we can know whether to speak of a particular pattern of sex-role differentiation in terms of hierarchy or complementarity is to see its relationship to other patterns of social differentiation that are less ambiguously understandable in terms of inequality; we may, for example, compare the patterns of interaction between men and women with those between individuals of the same sex but of different classes or ranks. We may inquire into the way in which gender serves as a metaphor for other modes of social asymmetry and vice versa.[11]

The comparative study of social inequality between the sexes depends upon the kind of research into gender symbolism that has been discussed above. Such research directs our attention to the symbolic component of social hierarchy and domination. As Kelly points out, beliefs like those the Etoro hold about witchcraft and sexual relations constitute "a mechanism for the production of an elementary system of inequality based on age and sex" (Kelly 1976: 51).

III. Gender and the Sociology of Knowledge

In the course of my own attempt to provide a general characterization of sexual hierarchy in a South American Indian society, mentioned earlier, I had occasion to consider men's and women's differential access to knowledge. In subsequent years, this issue has become a focus for ethnographic analysis and theoretical speculation. Anthropologists have come to think in terms not only of who controls the material means of production, but who dominates the means of symbolic production as well; they have raised the question of whether men and women who are members of the same society can be said to form "subcultures." In brief, gender studies have brought to the fore issues concerning the sociology of knowledge—a matter of central concern to the social sciences generally. Within anthropology, the approach to the sociology of knowledge has been largely in the Durkheimian mode, in which the internal homogeneity of societies is emphasized and shared representational systems are viewed as reflections of overall social structure. Sex-role studies have underlined the importance of internal social differentiation and its effects on what anthropologists refer to as "culture."

Recent ethnographic studies have shown that different pictures of the same society can emerge depending on whether one sees that society through the eyes of its male or its female members. One of the more influential of these studies is Jane Goodale's ethnography of marriage among the Tiwi, a northern Australian Aboriginal group (Goodale 1971). In the anthropological literature, marriage systems are generally analyzed from a male perspective. In showing us what the system looks like from the other side, Goodale is able to clarify certain features of kinship and marriage in an Australian society, making more comprehensible what has traditionally been one of the knottier areas of ethnography. (It is interesting to note that Goodale entitled her book *Tiwi Wives,* while an earlier ethnography of the Tiwi and their marriage system that focused on men and was written by two male ethnographers—Hart and Pilling 1960—was entitled simply *The Tiwi of Northern Australia.*)

It has been suggested in a number of recent studies that cultures of male dominance may, in fact, be men's cultures, not shared by women who have their own ideas about what is important in life. Some anthropologists have attempted to investigate the conditions for the emergence of a women's subculture and also to determine whether it functions to support or challenge the society's dominant values (see, for example, Murphy and Murphy 1974, Sutton et al. 1975, and Dwyer 1978).

Of all of the attempts that have thus far been made to apply a sociology of knowledge to sex-role studies, the one that has generated the most discussion is an article by Edwin Ardener, a British social anthropologist, entitled "Belief and the Problem of Women" (Ardener 1972). Ardener claims that it is generally males who control the mode of symbolic production in a society and are the major creators of its dominant world view; women's perspectives remain "muted." Ardener goes on to tie this difference in men's and women's world views to the problem of bias in ethnography by proposing that the models male informants provide are the kinds of models that will be understandable to social anthropologists (who are either men themselves or women who have presumably been socialized within a male-oriented intellectual tradition). According to Ardener, the analytic tools we have at hand as anthropologists do not prepare us to hear or understand the views held by women.[12]

The issue of male bias, raised in Ardener's critique of anthropological models of social structure and symbol systems, has received a considerable amount of attention in the literature on gender.[13] This concern over sex bias dovetails with a more general self-consciousness that has characterized the profession in recent years. Anthropologists have, at various times in the history of the discipline, shown a special sensitivity to the subjective dimension of ethnographic research. They have realized the need for learning how properties of the human recording instrument affect the record obtained. In the 1930s, when Freudian ideas were particularly influential in American society, it was sometimes suggested that anthropologists be psychoanalyzed before going into the field. The phase of self-awareness that anthropology has entered into more recently has developed within a different context—an amalgam of philosophical influences (notably, from the fields of phenomenology and hermeneutics) and the political auto-criticism of a profession that has belatedly acknowledged its relationship to colonialism.

Within this context of reflexiveness, we can investigate how gender, among other things, influences our perspectives as ethnographers. We are coming to understand how sex bias has skewed our vision in a number of areas, including human evolution. Unfortunately the effect of gender on scholarship is not always dealt with in as sophisticated a fashion as one might wish. For one thing, there is commonly a failure to distinguish consistently between sex bias emanating from the observer and sex bias characteristic of the community under study. A deeper and more complex problem has to do with the labeling of certain ideas as "male" or "female." It is one thing to identify the sex of someone who is expressing an idea or of the group most likely to benefit from it; determining authorship, however, is another matter, not to mention establishing a connection between gender and the form or content of the idea itself. Ardener's views on male bias, while containing some specific suggestions about the respective cosmological beliefs of men and women, are somewhat murky in their wider implications. Is it being suggested that the entire conceptual apparatus of anthropology is "male-oriented"? If so, how much of it must be totally reformulated, and what would the result look like? Are female ethnographers more likely than male ethnographers to develop a receptivity to the "muted" thought systems of women in the societies we study?

Implicit in many discussions of sex bias, and in much of the literature in women's studies more generally, is the assumption that only women can or should study women—what we might call the it-takes-one-to-know-one position. This attitude, prompted by a feminist awareness of the distorting views of women held by the largely male social scientific establishment, also finds support in the practicalities of field work; the division between men's and women's social worlds is sharply drawn in a large number of societies. Tendencies toward a sexual division of labor in our profession, however, require critical reflection more than they require epistemological justification or a new source of ideological support. After all, if it really took one to know one, the entire field of anthropology would be an aberration.

One of the more extreme statements on male bias (Rohrlich-Leavitt, Sykes, and Weatherford 1975) asserts that there is not only an anthropology of women, but an anthropology by women. The authors survey some of the respective contributions of male and female anthropologists to the study of Australian Aboriginal societies, and present a general theoretical argument to support their view that women are superior ethnographers. This article is of interest in that it develops explicitly certain assumptions that appear covertly in some of the other sex-role literature and, in so doing, reveals the confused and contradictory nature of these assumptions. First of all, Rohrlich-Leavitt et al. presume that a female anthropologist has the capacity to understand the subjective experience of her female informants just by virtue of the common sex bond, a highly questionable presumption. The woman ethnographer's ability to identify with her female informants is commended as an ability to achieve the insider's perspective (something men are said to be unable to do), while the male ethnographer's identification with his male informants is seen as bias (a disability to which women ethnographers are apparently immune). There is a certain piquancy in the reversal here: double standards of this sort, that operate through switching labels for the same thing, generally work against women. They are not, however, any more tenable when they work against men.

Rohrlich-Leavitt et al. maintain that women have a greater capacity not only for subjectivity but for objectivity as well — not the pseudo-objectivity of male anthropologists (which is seen as an alienating form of scientific manipulation), but an objectivity resulting from women's position as socially marginal. Women, by virtue of being an oppressed class that has to deal with a dominant class, achieve the kind of "double consciousness" that also characterizes economically exploited and racially stigmatized groups. The concept of double consciousness is an interesting one, but cannot be applied in a naive manner. In general, the issues dealt with by these anthropologists — the respective advantages and limitations of insiders' and outsiders' perspectives, the problem of objectivity and the question of whether one sub-group in society is more likely to possess it than another—have occupied the attention of major social theorists. We cannot consider the problem solved, but neither should we expend our efforts on trying to reinvent the wheel.

This brings me back to the general position I argued in the opening section of this paper: that gender studies should be integrated into mainstream social science research. Let me emphasize here that the process has to work both ways. The enduring contributions to gender studies are being made by those who are not only concerned with transforming the social sciences, but also able to make use of the major past accomplishments of their disciplines.

* * *

Recent sex-role studies have been characterized by a convergence of scholarly and political concerns. The energy generated by this merging of purposes has resulted not only in contributions to anthropological knowledge, but also in some welcome changes in the respective roles of women and men in the profession.

It may now be time for gender studies to move beyond the stage where scientific and scholarly goals were so closely tied to political and personal ones. There is generally some connection, to be sure, but we should seek to make that connection the subject of productive intellectual struggle rather than an influence leading us to adhere unreflectingly to a particular set of concerns. Several students of gender have come to worry about the extent to which we have been projecting our own historically specific situation onto the lives and experiences of those we study; we need to be receptive to encountering the unfamiliar in the field of gender studies, as in ethnographic research more generally.

The danger in too close an association between scholarship and social reformism is not only in the limits it places on intellectual inquiry, but also in the implication that our activities as social, moral, and political beings are dependent on what we are able to discover in our scientific research. Loosening the tie would have liberating consequences both for gender studies as an area of anthropological investigation and for feminism as a social movement. It is toward this stage that we are perhaps moving now.

NOTES

1. There were, to be sure, important earlier anthropological contributions to the cross-cultural study of gender, including the well-known work of Margaret Mead and the descriptions of sex role differentiation that can be found, to varying degrees, in most standard ethnographic monographs. With the exception of certain culture-and-personality anthropologists like Mead, however, and those few ethnographers who gave sex roles a central place in their descriptive work, gender was not considered an important focus for anthropological research and theorizing and did not mobilize the energies of large numbers of anthropologists until recently. In this discussion, I am concentrating on contributions that have come out of this more recent period.
2. A discussion of how markedness operates on various levels of language can be found in Lyons 1968. The term is first defined on pp. 79–80.
3. A similar point can be made about age. It would be interesting to trace the parallel development of a sociology of sex differences and a sociology of age differences.
4. I have had occasion to do a state-of-the-art survey in an earlier publication (Shapiro 1979). Other comprehensive review articles include Lamphere 1977, Quinn 1977, Rogers 1978, and Tiffany 1978.
5. As another Melanesianist has pointed out (Strathern 1981), Weiner is here doing something very similar to what Malinowski had done before her: setting up Trobriand man (or, in this case, woman), in opposition to Western man (or woman) as a model for humanity in general. This kind of secondary ethnocentrism is an occupational hazard of anthropology, an understandable outcome of the long, intense, and difficult business of trying to learn about another culture. Commonly labeled "Bongo-Bongoism," it paradoxically combines a habit of undermining generalizations because they do not happen to fit one's own ethnographic experience with a propensity of viewing the world at large from the vantage point of the particular society one has studied.
6. Rogers (1978:134–35) has noted that the association of women with nature and men with culture is not as straightforward even in our society as Ortner seems to indicate. A more extensive examination of the concepts of nature and culture in Western societies, and their development over time, can be found in various of the articles in MacCormack and Strathern 1980; other articles in this collection address the issue of how these concepts do or do not fit the world views of other societies.
7. Two important new contributions to this body of literature are the recently published set of essays edited by MacCormack and Strathern (1980) and a forthcoming collection of papers edited by Ortner and Whitehead (in press).
8. A more detailed exposition of Friedl's argument, and a discussion of similar approaches, can be found in Shapiro 1979: 270–77.
9. A comprehensive discussion of this issue, supported by data from different geographical regions, can be found in Boserup 1970.
10. Rosaldo (1980) has also made this general argument.

11. Strathern, for example, discusses how gender ranking serves as a means for expressing hierarchy among men in Melpa society (Highland New Guinea), and how the contrast between "big men" and "rubbish men," in turn, informs the way in which sexual asymmetry itself is viewed (Strathern 1976).
12. Shirley Ardener has edited a collection of ethnographic essays devoted to pursuing this line of investigation; Edwin Ardener's original article is reprinted in the volume (S. Ardener 1975).
13. Dickerson ([1980] n.d.) provides an overview of how the recent sex-role literature has dealt with the issue of male bias in anthropology, giving special attention to the various political and theoretical concerns that have motivated the inquiry. Milton (1979) and Strathern (in press) present detailed critiques of the concept of male bias and the uses to which it is put.

REFERENCES

Ardener, Edwin 1972. Belief and the Problem of Women. In J.S. LaFontaine (ed.) *The Interpretation of Ritual.* London: Tavistock. (reprinted in S. Ardener (ed.) 1975. *Perceiving Women.* New York: Wiley)
Ardener, Shirley G. (ed.) 1975. *Perceiving Women.* New York: Wiley.
Bateson, Gregory [1936] 1958. *Naven.* Stanford: Stanford University Press.
Boserup, Ester 1970. *Women's Role in Economic Development.* London: G. Allen and Unwin.
Chodorow, Nancy 1974. Family Structure and Feminine Personality. In M.Z. Rosaldo and L. Lamphere (eds.) *Woman, Culture, and Society.* Stanford: Stanford University Press.
Dickerson, Jeanette [1980] n.d. Sex Bias and Anthropology, paper prepared for Seminar on Sex Roles, Bryn Mawr College, Spring 1980.
Dwyer, Daisy Hilse 1978. Ideologies of Sexual Inequality and Strategies for Change in Male-Female Relations. *American Ethnologist* 5 (2): 227–40.
Friedl, Ernestine 1975. *Women and Men: An Anthropologist's View.* New York: Holt, Rinehart and Winston.
Goodale, Jane 1971. *Tiwi Wives: A Study of the Women of Melville Island, North Australia.* Seattle: University of Washington Press.
Hart, C.W.M. and Arnold Pilling 1960. *The Tiwi of North Australia.* New York: Holt, Rinehart and Winston.
Kelly, Raymond 1976. Witchcraft and Sexual Relations. In Paula Brown and Georgeda Buchbinder (eds.) *Man and Woman in the New Guinea Highlands.* Special publication of the American Anthropological Association, no. 8. Washington, D.C.: American Anthropological Association.
Lamphere, Louise 1977. Review Essay: Anthropology. *Signs* 2 (3): 612–27.
Leacock, Eleanor 1975. Class, Commodity, and the Status of Women. In Ruby Rohrlich-Leavitt (ed.) *Women Cross-Culturally: Change and Challenge.* Mouton: The Hague.
Lyons, John 1968. *Introduction to Theoretical Linguistics.* Cambridge: Cambridge University Press.
MacCormack, Carol and Marilyn Strathern (eds.) 1980. *Nature, Culture and Gender.* Cambridge: Cambridge University Press.
Milton, Kay 1979. Male Bias in Anthropology? *Man* 14 (1): 40–54.
Murphy, Yolanda and Robert F. Murphy 1974. *Women of the Forest.* New York: Columbia University Press.

O'Laughlin, Bridget 1974. Mediation of Contradictions: Why Mbum Women Do Not Eat Chicken. In M.Z. Rosaldo and L. Lamphere (eds.) *Woman, Culture, and Society.* Stanford: Stanford University Press.

Ortner, Sherry B. 1974. Is Female to Male as Nature is to Culture? In M.Z. Rosaldo and L. Lamphere (eds.) *Woman, Culture, and Society.* Stanford: Stanford University Press.

Ortner, Sherry and Harriet Whitehead (eds.) in press. *Sexual Meanings.* Cambridge: Cambridge University Press.

Quinn, Naomi 1977. Anthropological Studies on Women's Status. *Annual Review of Anthropology* 6: 182–222.

Rogers, Susan 1978. Women's Place: A Critical Review of Anthropological Theory. *Comparative Studies in Society and History* 20 (1): 123–62.

Rohrlich-Leavitt, Ruby, Barbara Sykes, and Elizabeth Weatherford 1975. Aboriginal Woman: Male and Female Anthropological Perspectives. In Ruby Rohrlich-Leavitt (ed.) *Women Cross-Culturally: Change and Challenge.* Mouton: The Hague.

Rosaldo, Michelle 1974. Woman, Culture, and Society: A Theoretical Overview. In M.Z. Rosaldo and L. Lamphere (eds.) *Woman, Culture, and Society.* Stanford: Stanford University Press.

Rosaldo, Michelle Z. 1980. The Use and Abuse of Anthropology: Reflections on Feminism and Cross-Cultural Understanding. *Signs* 5 (3): 389–417.

Rosaldo, Michelle Z. and Louise Lamphere (eds.) 1974. *Woman, Culture, and Society.* Stanford: Stanford University Press.

Shapiro, Judith 1972. *Sex Roles and Social Structure among the Yanomama Indians of Northern Brazil.* Ph.D. Dissertation, Department of Anthropology, Columbia University.

— — — 1976. Sexual Hierarchy among the Yanomama. In June Nash and Helen Safa (eds.) *Sex and Class in Latin America.* New York: Praeger.

— — — 1979. Cross-Cultural Perspectives on Sexual Differentiation. In Herant Katchadovrian (ed.) *Human Sexuality, A Comparative and Developmental Perspective.* Berkeley: University of California Press.

Strathern, Marilyn 1976. An Anthropological Perspective. In Barbara Lloyd and John Archer (eds.) *Exploring Sex Differences.* New York: Academic Press.

— — — 1981. Culture in a Netbag: The Manufacture of a Subdiscipline Anthropology, in *Man* (N.S.) 16.

Sutton, Constance, Susan Makiesky, Daisy Dwyer, and Laura Klein 1975. Women, Knowledge, and Power. In Ruby Rohrlich-Leavitt (ed.) *Women Cross-Culturally: Change and Challenge.* Mouton: The Hague.

Tiffany, Sharon 1978. Models and the Social Anthropology of Women: A Preliminary Assessment. *Man* 13 (1): 34–51.

Weiner, Annette 1976. *Women of Value, Men of Reknown.* Austin: University of Texas Press.

— — — 1979. Trobriand Kinship from Another View: The Reproductive Power of Women and Men. *Man* 14 (2): 328–48.

— — — 1980. Reproduction: A Replacement for Reciprocity. *American Ethnologist* 7 (1): 71–85.

CHANGING CONCEPTIONS OF MEN AND WOMEN:
A Psychologist's Perspective

JANET T. SPENCE

SCIENTIFIC THEORIES DO NOT ARISE out of a vacuum. At least at the beginning, theories about psychosocial phenomena that guide research and the interpretation of empirical evidence tend to be drawn from everyday, folk psychology. Conventional wisdom about the nature of human beings is typically an amalgam of shrewd common sense observation, myths based on ignorance or hangovers from the past, and ideology about what ought to be—a mixture of truths, half-truths, and falsehoods. When these belief systems are widely shared and reflect deeply entrenched values, they take on the aura of self-evident truths. Our beliefs become highly resistant to challenge, if only out of blank incomprehension that alternatives are possible.

Considered dispassionately, folk wisdom is probably as good a source of psychological hypotheses as any in initial stages of inquiry. Despite their quite genuine commitments to objectivity, however, psychologists (like all scientists, as Kuhn has so compellingly argued) are products of the society in which they were born and reared and are not immune to being swept up in its world views. It is all too easy to treat the folk wisdom of one's

Janet T. Spence, whose Ph.D. is from the University of Iowa, is Ashbel Smith Professor of Psychology and Educational Psychology at the University of Texas at Austin. Her current research is focused on masculinity, femininity, and sex-roles, and on achievement motivation, particularly as it relates to women's achievement. Her publications include the book (with Robert L. Helmreich) *Masculinity and Femininity: Their Psychological Dimensions, Correlates, and Antecedents*, 1978.

Preparation of this article was supported in part by National Science Foundation Grant Number BNS 78-03911 and NIMH Grant Number MH32066, Janet T. Spence and Robert L. Helmreich, Principal Investigators.

society as axiomatic truths, failing to recognize that these "truths" are in fact hypotheses that must be subjected to empirical verification and that it is necessary to articulate fully the premises on which these hypotheses are based. In the absence of explicit statements about the assumptions underlying psychological models, there is a failure to gather the data that might permit them to be challenged or to consider theoretical alternatives that might be more faithful to the empirical realities.

No better illustration may be found than the conceptions of men and women and their roles that until quite recently dominated psychological thinking and, in certain key respects, continue to do so. Examination of earlier work from the vantage point of the 1980s suggests that, although there was often theoretical disagreement about specific gender-related phenomena, these theories nonetheless shared several core assumptions, assumptions that research conducted over the past decade indicates correspond to those of the general public. Before describing these presuppositions, I will sketch rapidly the social context in which they are embedded.

Divisions of labor cleaving along lines of gender are universal in human societies, men and women being assigned different duties, responsibilities, and statuses. The particulars and sharpness of sex-role distinctions vary from one society to another and, in response to changes in social and natural forces to which a society is subject, from one historical period to another. A feature common to many societies, however, has been aptly captured by Talcott Parsons' distinction between instrumental and expressive functions (Parsons & Bales, 1955). Men are assigned the primary responsibility for their society's political, economic, and intellectual institutions, and for providing their families with leadership and economic support. Women, on the other hand, are assigned the primary responsibility for maintaining the home, caring for the children, and providing emotional support to family members. The sexes are also expected to differ in a myriad of other ways, some unique to particular societies and temporally unstable and others more nearly universal: body movements, style of dress, manner of speech, social behavior as codified in rules of social etiquette, vocational and avocational interests, sexual orientation and behavior, and so forth. These behaviors, many of which carry with them positive and negative sanctions for role conformity or violation, are designed to emphasize the distinctiveness of the sexes and serve to maintain the different status accorded to men and women.

I

One of the central assumptions that until recently underlay psychological approaches to men and women has been that the collectivity of socially sanctioned behaviors and attributes which a given society has defined as "masculine" or "feminine" form a single, bipolar dimension.

To amplify this statement, an operative principle has been that the appearance of "masculine" or "feminine" behaviors and attributes are substantially correlated across individuals of each sex. In effect, one can use information about a given type of gender-related behavior to make inferences about the degree to which the individual manifests other "masculine" and "feminine" characteristics. In males, for example, "limp wrists" and interest in certain occupations such as hairdressing or interior decoration have often been considered diagnostic signs of homosexuality, whereas in females, the appearance of "masculine" personality traits such as tough-mindedness and assertiveness have been regarded as signs of rejection of the entire female role. This presumed association of the individual components of "masculinity" and "femininity" further implies that that which is more characteristic of males than females in a given society is by definition *nonfeminine*, and that which is more characteristic of females than males in that society is *nonmasculine*; masculinity and femininity are held as mirror-images of each other. On a more conceptual level, a single underlying dimension is implied, a dimension given such labels as masculinity-femininity or sex-role identification. Individuals, male and female, can be assigned a position along this hypothetical dimension, to indicate *how much* of this psychological property they possess, with most males expected to cluster at one end and most females expected to cluster at the other. Although recognizing that some variability can be expected among "normal" men and women, this conception implies that sex-linked psychological characteristics are essentially dimorphic, in the manner of biological gender.

This unidimensional conception and the assumptions it demands have rarely been explicitly proposed, but the ubiquity of the bipolar approach can easily be demonstrated. For example, until recently there has been unquestioned acceptance of so-called "masculinity-femininity" tests, objective self-report instruments in which respondents are asked to describe their psychological characteristics, preferences, and behaviors. No theoretical rationale or conceptual definition has guided item selection for such psychometric instruments, save for the criterion that item responses distinguish empirically between men and women and, in one well-known scale, the additional capacity of item responses to distinguish between homosexuals and heterosexuals (Constantinople, 1973). Further, each individual's responses yield a single score, representing the individual's position along the hypothetical masculinity-femininity continuum. Still another example may be found in the use of measures of limited manifest content, such as masculine vs. feminine toy preferences in children or self-concepts of certain gender-related personality traits in older individuals, to infer some hypothetical unitary property such as degree of "sex-role identity." Indeed, the pervasiveness of the unidimensional assumption is reflected in the linguistic convention that has been almost universally adopted in psychology of substituting the term "sex roles" to refer to psychological sex differences in general (except, perhaps, for cognitive abilities), therefore broadening the technical definition of "roles" beyond recognition. If the unidimensional assumption were valid, this verbal equation of "sex roles" with "sex differences" would be harmless and the methods of measuring "masculinity-femininity," "sex-role identification," and the like that I described above would be acceptable. However, recent evidence has failed to confirm the implications of this bipolar model.

Causal as well as correlational links have sometimes been assumed between specific components of sex-related phenomena. Instances are relatively infrequent and subtle in modern psychology but were more common in earlier times and can still be found in the lay public. One particularly blatant example is amusing from the safety of the 1980s but might serve as a cautionary tale for our own time. Through much of the nineteenth century, respected scientific opinion held that women were not merely men's intellectual inferiors but could hardly be said to have a "mind" at all. When pressures began to build late in the nineteenth century to allow women access to the same secondary school and college curricula as men, a hue and cry arose that, except for a few deviants, women not only were incapable of mastering such material, let alone of entering business and the professions, but also would literally become physically unsexed if they attempted to indulge in masculine intellectual pursuits. One "authority," for example, confidently asserted that the "mental woman" would become gaunt and bony and that her breasts would shrink! (See Ehrenreich & English, 1979 for a review of these theories.) Contemporary echoes of this thinking can still be found. For example, an army general, a former chairman of the Joint Chiefs of Staff, was widely quoted when women were about to be admitted to West Point, as saying that only a few "freaks" were capable of keeping up with the male cadets and that if women attempted to do so, they would become "masculinized." Fortunately, as I have noted, one rarely finds in more recent scientific accounts the unsupportable assumption that manipulating one component of the masculinity-femininity package will necessarily have strong and direct effects on others.

A second pervasive assumption in psychological conceptions of males and females has been that there are core distinctions between the psychological make-up of the sexes that contribute to the maintenance and perpetuation of sex-role systems in which men have greater power and control over resources than women.

While early scientific theories placed heavy reliance on the innate intellectual inferiority of females, to justify denying them equal status with men, psychologists have taken the lead over the past half-century in demonstrating that men and women are similar in overall intellectual competence. Current evidence (e.g., Maccoby & Jacklin, 1974) suggests that although the sexes may differ in specific cognitive abilities, sex differences are at best minor in magnitude and do not uniformly favor one sex.

Psychological theorists have continued to assert, however, that the sexes differ in *temperamental* qualities. Such outer-directed and self-assertive attributes as independence, decisiveness, aggressiveness, and capacity for leadership are attributed to males, and such inner-directed and interpersonally sensitive qualities as emotionality, gentleness, and awareness of others' feelings are attributed to females.

Hypotheses about sex differences in personality characteristics of this sort are to be found in various guises in a number of theories, and the distinctions between the sexes have been given various labels. The most common are masculine *instrumentality* and feminine *expressiveness,* terms that parallel those devised by Talcott Parsons to describe masculine versus feminine roles and that serve to emphasize the purported relationship between these personal attributes and role enactment. Men, in order to discharge their onerous instrumental role responsibilities properly, must be abundantly endowed with these self-assertive, goal-directed characteristics. Similarly, women must possess nurturant, interpersonally oriented characteristics to discharge their domestic, intrafamilial responsibilities.

Roles are complementary. If normative expectations are that men be dominant and exercise leadership over women, then women's expected role is to follow and be submissive. This complementarity of *roles* has perhaps encouraged the assumption that the clusters of personal qualities presumed to facilitate successful role enactment are psychological opposites. In any event, psychological theories of the past, like the "common sense" notions of the general public, have typically taken for granted that the degree of instrumentality an individual possesses is negatively correlated with his or her degree of expressiveness.

Thus, as with other gender-differentiating phenomena, a single bipolar continuum has been implied, the "masculine" pole representing the presence of instrumental characteristics and the relative absence of expressive characteristics and the "feminine" pole representing the reverse pattern of attributes. In conjunction with the assumption I outlined earlier—namely that all sex-differentiating phenomena are related and reflect a single underlying property—this conception further implies that knowledge of individuals' positions on this masculine-feminine personality dimension allows inferences to be made about them with respect to other gender-differentiating attributes and role-related behaviors.

The etiology of these presumed sex differences in instrumental and expressive traits and related characteristics has been a matter of continuous dispute. At one extreme are theorists who propose that their origins are completely to be found in the socialization pressures to which each sex has been subject and in the different life experiences of men and women throughout the life cycle. At the other extreme are theorists of a sociobiological persuasion who postulate that biological factors are also heavily implicated. According to these theorists, genetically determined sex-differences in temperamental qualities have not only shaped the evolution of sex-role systems but are sufficiently great and lacking in malleability as to constrain the social arrangements that a society could reasonably devise (Archer, 1976).

Whether or not they stressed the contribution of biological factors in bringing about differences in the psychological make-up of men and women, past theories accepted traditional sex-role divisions as givens. Thus, the third assumption that dominated psychological conceptions of the sexes was that, in overall outline, conventional role distinctions were, if not inevitable, then at least nonproblematic.

One final assumption can be outlined with equal brevity. Sex-typing in normatively expected behaviors and attributes was presumed to be associated with superior psychological adjustment and mental health. While some variation was permitted and expected among "normal" men and women, the range of tolerable deviations from accepted standards was assumed to be relatively small. Discontent with one's assigned roles or conspicuous deviations from expected standards in one's attributes and behaviors were assumed to be pathological in and of themselves as well as symptomatic of an underlying personality disturbance.

Earlier acceptance of the *status quo* within psychology is revealed not only by examining the theoretical writings and empirical investigations of the time but also by observing what was *not* being done. Throughout much of psychology's history, most areas of the discipline have been relatively oblivious to questions relating to the nature of men and women and the relationships between the sexes. With certain exceptions (such as the concern of child psychologists with the development of "sex-role identification") not only were relatively few investigations devoted to these topics, but analyses of social-psychological studies published during the 1950s and 1960s have revealed that men were employed as subjects disproportionately more often than women (e.g., Holmes & Jorgeson, 1971). Occasionally, the rationale for preferring males was made explicit. For example, in the early studies arising from Atkinson's (1958) highly influential expectancy-value theory of achievement motivation, done in the 1950s, data obtained from males but not females were consistent with theoretical prediction. These findings led to the conclusion that women's achievement motives differed from men's (McClelland, 1966) with the result that in the following decade or so, males were used as subjects almost exclusively. In most studies, however, no explanation for employing only males was given, but the conclusion is unavoidable that males tended to be regarded (by investigators who were almost always male) as the norm or the standard sex. Women, in contrast, were more of an exotic species, outside the norm, and less important to study, except perhaps as a curiosity.

II

The development of social concern with the status of women initiated by passage of the 1964 Civil Rights Act and the rise of the feminist movement in the late 1960s brought a rapid end to psychologists' neglect of topics related to gender, and over the course of the last decade, has led to a reexamination of our conceptions of men and women. Along with members of other disciplines, psychologists writing from a feminist perspective have questioned the usefulness of our conventional sex-role structure and have pointed both to the injustice of any system in which power and prestige are so unevenly divided between the sexes and to the destructive effects of these inequities, particularly on women. Along with these challenges, the 1970s ushered in attacks on the proposition that masculinity and femininity are mirror images, end-points of a single continuum (e.g., Constantinople, 1973; Block, 1973; Bem, 1974; Spence, Helmreich, & Stapp, 1975). These revisionist views and the empirical research they generated have brought to prominence a conception of masculinity and femininity as separate and independent dimensions. This hypothesis suggests that while men in general are more "masculine" than women, and women in general are more "feminine" than men, members of both sexes not only can, but often *do*, exhibit a high degree of *both* masculine and feminine characteristics and behaviors. The term that has come to be used to designate the co-occurrence of masculine and feminine attributes is *androgyny*.[1]

Within psychology, the term androgyny was first introduced by Sandra Bem, whose work has also done much to popularize the concept. Because her ideas not only are influential within psychology but also represent, in some critical respects, the most articulate expression of certain widely held conceptualizations, I will outline her theoretical proposals in some detail.

Bem has been admirably frank in acknowledging her ideological biases and political goals. "[M]y purpose," she has written, "has always been a feminist one: to help free the human personality from the restricting prison of sex-role stereotyping and to develop a conception of mental health which is free from culturally imposed definitions of masculinity and femininity" (Bem, 1978, p. 4).

The new ideal that she initially proposed was the androgyne. The androgynous individual, in contrast to the rigidly masculine male and feminine female, is comfortable exhibiting behaviors associated with either the male or the female role as appropriate to requirements of the situation and, as needed, is capable of integrating both masculine and feminine qualities into single acts. This type of behavioral flexibility, her model implies, is in itself desirable and is related to social effectiveness, not merely in some utopia of the future but in the reality of the present. Further, greater mental health and personal adjustment are associated with the androgynous condition and not with traditional sex-typing.

To test these hypotheses—that masculinity and femininity are independent dimensions so that it is possible for a given individual to be both masculine and feminine in his or her attributes and behaviors and that the androgynous individual who combines both sets of qualities is better adjusted and more socially effective than others—Bem developed a self-report measure, the Bem Sex Role Inventory (BSRI; Bem, 1974). The BSRI includes two major categories of items, masculine and feminine. Masculine items were intended to refer to qualities whose presence is commonly believed to be more desirable in males than females. As it turned out, items on the Masculinity scale largely (but not exclusively) describe what I earlier identified as desirable instrumental characteristics (e.g., ambitious, assertive, independent), whereas items on the Femininity scale largely describe desirable expressive characteristics (e.g., affectionate, gentle, sensitive to the needs of others).

In confirmation of the speculations of psychological theorists as well as of stereotypes held by the man and woman on the street, Bem (1974) reported that men as a group scored higher on the Masculinity scale and lower on the Femininity scale than women. The finding that at that time was considered startling was that, *within* each sex, the relationship between scores on the two scales was essentially orthogonal, rather than negative as demanded by prior theories. These data led to the conclusion not only that androgyny—the possession of a high degree of both masculine and feminine qualities—was theoretically possible but also that a substantial number of androgynous men and women could actually be identified. Similar results have also been found with the Personal Attributes Questionnaire (PAQ; Spence, Helmreich, & Stapp, 1974; Spence & Helmreich, 1978), a self-report instrument developed by my colleagues and myself that is similar to the BSRI but, in its current form, contains by design only socially desirable instrumental and expressive traits on its Masculinity and Femininity scales, respectively.

Evidence bearing on the hypothesis that androgyny, as defined by the BSRI or the PAQ, leads to superior personal adjustment and social effectiveness has yielded equivocal results. But it has *unambiguously* been shown that in women as well as in men, high scores on the *Masculinity* scales of these instruments are substantially associated with indices of effective functioning (e.g., Spence, et al., 1975; Spence & Helmreich, 1978). Sex-typed women—these who score relatively high on the Femininity scale and relatively low on Masculinity—do not fare as well as their androgynous or masculine sisters. With these seemingly revolutionary demonstrations in hand, the concept of androgyny gained instant prominence.

In her recent writings, Bem (1981) has highlighted another aspect of the rationale of the BSRI and has introduced another concept into her theoretical model, saliency of gender schema. Schema, according to cognitive psychologists, are cognitive structures consisting of networks of associations that serve to organize and guide the interpretation of information. Every human society, Bem observes, teaches its members a diverse network of associations linked to concepts of "masculinity" and "femininity." The stress that society places on the importance of gender turns this network into cognitive schema that lead the individual to organize and process diverse kinds of information in gender terms, including information about the self. Bem's specific contribution to gender schema theory is that individuals differ in the strength or the saliency of their gender schema — the importance they attach to considerations of gender as a guide to their own behavior and the prominence of gender in determining their perceptions of the world around them.

The measure that Bem (1981) uses to identify individual differences in saliency of gender schemata is the BSRI, the self-report instrument described above. Sex-typed men and women, those who show opposite configurations of high and low scores on the Masculinity and Femininity scales, are assumed to be most strongly guided in the cognitive organization of their self-concepts and their perception of their world by gender schemata. Although Bem's theory of gender schema is recent, it was presaged in her treatment of the BSRI as a measure of "sex-roles" or "sex-role orientation," global concepts that imply that individuals vary in the degree to which their role behaviors and their perceptions of their personal attributes correspond to the social ideal of manliness or womanliness.

In its overall configurations, this gender-schema hypothesis resembles established theories of sex-role identification (Bronfenbrenner, 1960; Maccoby, 1966) in which it is proposed that children learn to identify with particular members of their own sex, such as their mothers or fathers, or with members of their own sex in general, and attempt to adopt the characteristics and values of these models. They thus acquire an appropriately masculine or feminine self-image and behave in the manner expected by society for members of their sex. Identification theorists, however, have typically taken the legitimacy of normatively expected distinctions between the sexes as a *given,* and thus assume that the acquisition of a firm sense of sex-role identification is a necessary component of normal development. Bem takes the opposite position. In a just society in which both men and women would be able to realize their full human potential, sex-role distinctions would be abolished and the importance of gender as an organizing principle would be reduced to a minimum. But, she notes, androgyny contains the seeds of its own destruction. As men and women approach this ideal state, attributes and behaviors will no longer be labeled as masculine or feminine but simply as human, and sex-roles will have been transcended (Hefner, Rebecca, & Olefshansky, 1975).

How widely this vision of a sex-blind society has been endorsed by feminists is unclear and even its proponents have yet to provide a scenario for such a society. Radically different scripts could be developed, depending on the assumptions one makes about the nature of other political, social, and economic institutions and the state of technology. Working out a diversity of models and the assumptions that each would require might be a fascinating and enlightening exercise but, to my knowledge, it is one that has never been systematically attempted.

The more purely scientific portions of "androgyny theory," however, immediately found an enthusiastic audience. Predictably, a critical backlash has also developed. One vocal critic (Sampson, 1977) has denounced the androgynous ideal as "selfish," encouraging men and women to be individually sufficient unto themselves, rather than cooperative and interdependent. The deleterious effects on the self of weakening sex-role or gender identity have been mentioned by other critics and the merits of the traditional family have been vigorously defended by still others. A host of other methodological and conceptual models have also begun to appear whose very diversity make them impossible to summarize. Those sympathetic to "androgyny theory" have also begun to express confusion, particularly about how androgyny is to be defined and about such seemingly technical matters as to how such instruments as the BSRI and the PAQ are to be scored to yield a measure of "androgyny."

III

Careful analysis suggests that a major source of our current theoretical disorder can be traced to our half-heartedness in throwing off conceptual legacies from the past. More particularly, we have placed an impossible explanatory burden on self-images of instrumentality and expressiveness as personal qualities. To explicate this contention, I will again return to Bem's widely accepted theories and to work with the BSRI and similar instruments, because they so neatly reflect the conceptual problems.

I noted at the beginning of this presentation that in work done prior to the development of the concept of androgyny, "masculinity" and "femininity" were never clearly defined, beyond a composite of everything that empirically or in normative expectations distinguished between men and women in a given society. Definitions of androgyny are no less vague, and have in fact taken only informal forms. Bem's description has served as the prototype: androgynous people are "*both* masculine and feminine, *both* assertive and yielding, *both* instrumental and expressive—depending on the situational appropriateness of these behaviors" (Bem, 1974, p. 155).

This description, which has been widely adopted, is remarkably content free, except for the illustrative references to expressive and instrumental traits. However, one can infer not only from this definition but also from the mixed content of the BSRI and the theory in which it is embedded that two global unidimensional constructs are being proposed. Instead of a single bipolar continuum, masculinity-femininity, there are two separate dimensions, masculinity *and* femininity. Within each category, all the characteristics and behaviors designated by society as "masculine" or as "feminine" tend to occur together and each specific characteristic serves as a diagnostic sign of a single underlying property, "masculinity" or "femininity." Instrumental and expressive traits are central features, but not the *only* features of "masculinity" and "femininity"; these latter concepts are clearly intended to specify global properties of the individual that *need* not be defined further.

Those who endorse this view of "androgyny" as possession of both masculinity and femininity in this global sense have commonly accepted at the same time that, from a joint consideration of individuals' degree of "masculinity" and degree of "femininity," one can also infer their degree of "sex-role identification" or the centrality of their use of gender schema, concepts that imply the extent to which individuals adhere to conventional images of their sex in their self-concepts, behaviors, and reactions to others. In this context, androgynous men and women have been described as having a weaker degree of sex-role identification or gender saliency than sex-typed individuals (that is, men who are high in masculinity but low in femininity and women who are high in femininity but low in masculinity). Superficially, these two sets of ideas appear to be mutually compatible. Closer inspection indicates, however, that they are in fundamental disagreement, containing a contradiction that has contributed to our theoretical disarray. What is implied by such concepts as sex-role orientation and saliency of gender schema is a *single, quantitative* dimension. At one end of the dimension are sex-typed individuals who are highly identified with their sex and have strong gender schema. Depending on other assumptions, the other extreme is marked either by individuals who are not sex-typed or by cross-sexed individuals, identified with the opposite sex. In the latter instance, those who are not sex-typed fall at the center of the distribution. But how is one to reconcile hypotheses that state that masculinity and femininity simultaneously form a *single dimension* and *two independent dimensions?*

This dilemma is starkly illustrated in the different methods that have been used to combine scores on the Masculinity and Femininity scales of the BSRI and thus to define "androgyny" operationally. In her initial studies, Bem used a subtractive procedure in which the difference between respondents' Masculinity and Femininity scores was obtained, with androgynous individuals being defined as those whose scores fell at the middle of the distribution, i.e., "balanced" individuals whose scores on the two scales were approximately equal, irrespective of absolute level. This procedure, which in essence is identical to that used in the traditional masculinity-femininity tests that were supposedly being discredited, produces a single distribution of scores, as called for by interpretation of the scores as a measure of a single global construct such as sex-role identification or saliency of gender. It is *incompatible,* however, with the notion of masculinity and femininity as independent dimensions. This latter hypothesis was empirically supported, of course, by the lack of correlation between masculinity and femininity scores. Further, the difference-score method employs an *operational* definition of androgyny — that it is a *balance* between masculinity and femininity scores whatever their absolute levels — that is in conflict with the nominal definition of androgyny that implies the possession of a *high degree* of both masculine and feminine characteristics.

In our initial studies (Spence, et al., 1975), my colleagues and I demonstrated that scoring schemes that take absolute scores into account and thus reflect the demonstrated statistical independence of the two scales on the BSRI and PAQ have greater predictive utility than the difference-score method. As a simple heuristic device for describing various score combinations, we suggested a four-category scheme based on the median split. Individuals relatively high in both masculinity and femininity scores are called Androgynous, thus bringing the operational definition of the term in line with the accepted verbal one. Individuals relatively high in Masculinity scores and relatively low in Femininity scores are labeled Masculine (and represent sex-typed males and cross-typed females), whereas individuals showing the opposite pattern are called Feminine (and represent sex-typed females and cross-sex males). Lastly, for lack of a better label, individuals scoring *low* on both dimensions are called Undifferentiated. Bem (1977) and her followers subsequently abandoned the difference-score method in favor of absolute-scoring methods such as the categorical scheme I just described, and they adopted as the operational definition of Androgyny relatively high scores on the Masculinity and Femininity scales. This scoring method, it is crucial to note, does *not* produce a single distribution of scores or an ordered series of groups. Nor, from the perspective of masculinity and femininity as independent dimensions, *should* it produce these outcomes.

But now consider the theoretical interpretation of the BSRI and other similar instruments that Bem (1981) currently favors, saliency of gender schema, or other unitary concepts such as sex-role identification. The lack of congruence between the demands of hypothesis and scoring scheme is now corrected. The gender-schema hypothesis specifies a single dimension, but the method for scoring the BSRI to indicate strength of these schema does not produce an ordering of the groups representing various combinations of masculinity and femininity. Masculine men and Feminine women clearly are assumed to have strong gender schema, but how are the Androgynous, Cross-typed, and Undifferentiated groups to be ordered?

The contradictions between these scoring schemes illustrate on an empirical level the contradictions on a theoretical level of simultaneously proposing that the same measure reflects one dimension and a pair of independent dimensions. Since both propositions cannot be valid, the only solution is to renounce one of them—or both of them.

According to the theoretical model proposed by my colleagues and myself (e.g., Spence & Helmreich, 1978, 1979), *both* propositions are in conspicuous need of repair. The proposal that masculinity and femininity are separate dimensions, once regarded as a revolutionary step forward, is as erroneous in its way as the theory it was intended to replace.

What we empirically label masculinity and femininity, I noted earlier, refers to a diverse collection of attributes and behaviors. Contrary to the powerful mind-set that has taught us to believe that "masculinity" or "femininity" in one component in this collectivity is symptomatic of other masculine or feminine behaviors and attributes, inspection of a rapidly expanding body of data suggests an incredibly complicated multidimensionality. Some gender-related phenomena involve single bipolar dimensions and others, two independent dimensions. Some kinds of gender-related behaviors and attributes are highly associated and others have little or no association. There are many "masculinities" and "femininities" and many kinds of "androgyny".

Because of the pivotal role instrumentality and expressiveness have played in theoretical conceptions of men and women, my colleagues and I have chosen to focus our theoretical and empirical efforts on the personality dimensions of these qualities, using the Personal Attributes Questionnaire as our measuring device. Some of the data obtained with this instrument may be used to illustrate the complexity with which we are faced. Psychometric analyses suggest that these clusters of socially desirable instrumental and expressive traits do form independent, unitary dimensions. "Androgyny," with respect to these *specific* gender-related trait constellations, is thus a viable concept. The data also suggest that, within each sex, self-concepts of instrumentality and expressiveness have important implications for other attributes and socially significant behaviors, some of them role-related. For example, marital dissatisfaction is more likely in couples in which both partners are sex-typed in personality (i.e., the husband is relatively high in instrumentality and relatively low in expressiveness and the wife is the reverse) than in couples showing other combinations of personality traits; whereas, marital satisfaction is particularly likely in androgynous couples (e.g., Antill, submitted for publication). On the other hand, the relationships of these personality variables to many role-related phenomena are often small and/or complex; for example, instrumentality and expressiveness are minimally related in both sexes to sex-role attitudes and many sex-role preferences and behaviors (e.g., Spence & Helmreich, 1978; Spence, Helmreich, and Sawin, 1980). Important as these personality dimensions may be, sex differences in instrumentality and expressiveness cannot be used as a major justification or explanation of sex-role behaviors at the level of the individual or for the perpetuation of our traditional sex-role system at the level of society. The task that remains before us is to develop more refined conceptualizations of gender-related phenomena so that the painstaking work of determining their antecedents, consequences, and interrelationships can proceed.

By way of summary, I will return to the assumptions, outlined earlier, that for so long shaped psychologists' theoretical conceptions and channeled their empirical research, and I will comment on their contemporary status. The day is long since past in which any serious scholar can accept as given either the contemporary reality or the desirability of a role system in which women are by force of custom and law relegated to the home and to subordinate status. In our society as a whole, no consensus has as yet emerged as to what further changes in our sex-role system are biologically feasible, sociologically likely, or psychologically desirable, but these are matters of open debate and no longer closed-off conclusions. We are uncertain about what produces the best "adjusted" members of each sex but we no longer accept that our goal as educators, parents, and psychologists is necessarily to produce the quintessence of stereotyped "masculinity" and "femininity" in our male and female children.

To this reader of the literature, the evidence overwhelmingly indicates that gender-related phenomena are multidimensional. Neither the conception that they form a single continuum—masculinity-femininity, sex-role identification, saliency of gender schema—nor the conception that they form two continua—masculinity and femininity—seem supportable. But old mind-sets die hard, and even among those who propose "androgyny" as the model for the future, there is constant backsliding into some type of single dimension conceptualization. Adherents to the multidimensional viewpoint are only slowly being won.

What, more specifically, is the status of such time-honored, unidimensional constructs as sex-role identification or such newer constructs as gender schema? Whether one supports or rejects the proposal that, in an ideal society, the importance of gender should be minimized, the observation that in contemporary society gender is a central organizing principle in men's and women's images of themselves and in their construction of their social world is indisputable. But attempts to "find" men's and women's sense of their own masculinity or femininity in specific sets of "masculine" and "feminine" behaviors and attributes have failed. If this sense does not lie in those properties our society defines as "masculine" and "feminine", where does it lie? Perhaps it is some ineffable, existential sense that like the elusive Scarlet Pimpernel, is found here, there, everywhere, and nowhere.

NOTES

1. Androgyny, which comes from the Greek words for male and female, initially was a little used synonym for hermaphroditism. Its use as a psychological term, however, has a long literary tradition. Samuel Coleridge, for example, wrote over a century ago, "The truth is, a great mind must be androgynous." However, it remained for feminist scholars writing within the past decade (e.g., Carolyn Heilbrun in *Toward a Recognition of Androgyny*, published in 1973) to make the term familiar and to broaden its accepted meanings to include psychological qualities.

REFERENCES

Antill, J. Sex-role complementarity vs. similarity in married couples. Submitted for publication.
Archer, J. Biological explanation of psychological sex differences. In B. Lloyd & J. Archer (Eds.), *Exploring Sex Differences*. London: Academic Press, 1976.
Atkinson, J.W. (Ed.), *Motives in Fantasy, Action and Society*. Princeton: Van Nostrand, 1958.
Bem, S.L. The measurement of psychological androgyny. *Journal of Consulting and Clinical Psychology*, 1974, *42*, 155–62.
Bem, S.L. Beyond androgyny: Some presumptuous prescriptions for a liberated sexual identity. In J.A. Sherman, & F.L. Denmark (Eds.), *The Psychology of Women: Future Directions in Research*. New York: Psychological Dimensions, Inc. 1978.
Bem, S.L. Gender schema theory: a cognitive account of sex typing. *Psychological Review*, 1981, *88*, 354–64.
Block, J.H. Conceptions of sex roles: Some cross-cultural and longitudinal perspectives. *American Psychologist*, 1973, *28*, 512–26.
Bronfenbrenner, U. Freudian theories of identification and their derivatives. *Child Development*, 1960, *31*, 15–40.
Constantinople, A. Masculinity-femininity: An exception to the famous dictum? *Psychological Bulletin*, 1973, *80*, 389–407.
Ehrenreich, B., & English, D. *For Her Own Good: 150 Years of the Expert's Advice to Women*. Garden City, N.Y.: Anchor Press/Doubleday, 1979.
Hefner, R., Rebecca, M., & Olefshansky, B. Development of sexual transcendence. *Human Development*, 1975, *18*, 143–58.
Holmes, D.S., & Jorgeson, B.W. Do personality and social psychologists study men more than women? *Representative Research in Social Psychology*, 1971, *2*, 71–76.
Maccoby, E.E. *The Development of Sex Differences*, E.E. Maccoby (Ed.), Stanford University Press, Stanford, CA., 1966.

148

Maccoby, E. E., & Jacklin, C. N. *The Psychology of Sex Differences.* Stanford: Stanford University Press, 1974.

McClelland, D. C. Longitudinal trends in the relation of thought to action. *Journal of Clinical and Consulting Psychology,* 1966, *30,* 479–83.

Parsons, T., & Bales, R. F. *Family Socialization and Interaction Process.* Glencoe: Free Press, 1955.

Sampson, E. E. Psychology and the American ideal. *Journal of Personality and Social Psychology,* 1977, *35,* 767–82.

Spence, J. T., & Helmreich, R. L. *Masculinity and Femininity: Their Psychological Dimensions, Correlates and Antecedents.* Austin: The University of Texas Press, 1978.

Spence, J. T., Helmreich, R. L., & Stapp, J. Ratings of self and peers on sex-role attributes and their relation to self-esteem and conceptions of masculinity and femininity. *Journal of Personality and Social Psychology,* 1975, *32,* 29–39.

Spence, J. T., Helmreich, R. L., & Stapp, J. The Personal Attributes Questionnaire: A measure of sex-role stereotypes and masculinity-femininity. JSAS *Catalog of Selected Documents in Psychology,* 1974, *4,* 43.

Spence, J. T., Helmreich, R. L., & Sawin, L. L. The Male-Female Relations Questionnaire: A self-report inventory of sex-role behaviors and preferences and its relationships to masculine and feminine personality traits, sex role attitudes, and other measures. JSAS *Catalog of Selected Documents,* 1980, *10,* 87.

WOMEN IN SOCIOLOGICAL ANALYSIS:
New Scholarship Versus Old Paradigms

THE SELECTIVE EYE of sociology, like the selective eyes of political science, economics, philosophy, and psychology, has been blind to women for decades. Description and analysis of the role of women in these disciplines was neglected; thus, half of the world was left out, and incomplete and wrong assessments of human behavior were conveyed. When only men's work and behavior were studied or assessed, we had only a partial knowledge of the occupational stratification and political systems, and indeed we had only skewed insights into human nature. It was impossible to learn much about women, let alone people and the social system, from the myopic views of social scientists and social philosophers. Even assumptions about the interface between biology, sociology, and psychology were muddied by inappropriate, unscientific assumptions. Social scientists measured as real, qualities like "masculinity" and "femininity," which were often only the artifacts of underlying and unproven assumptions, reifications of those concepts.

The neglect or misinterpretation of women in the social sciences and the attendant damage it did to the various disciplines and to women goes far back in social thought. Respected scientists and philosophers made women victims of incorrect assessments of their natures, psyches, or proper place. Susan Moller Okin, in a recent book, *Women in Western Political Thought*,[1] shows how the suppression of women's rights has been

Cynthia Fuchs Epstein is professor of Sociology at Queens College and the Graduate Center of the City University of New York. She is Co-Director of the Program in Sex Roles and Social Change at Columbia University. Her most recent book is *Women in Law*, based on a 15-year study of women in the legal profession.

legitimized since the golden age of Athens, despite social philosophers' arguments for the rights of people in general. Thus, thinkers from Aristotle and Rousseau to Talcott Parsons and Erik Erikson in our day have maintained that women are more limited than men and therefore more suited to the domestic than the public sphere. Curiously, Plato's and John Stuart Mill's confidence in women's capacity to perform the social tasks of men, such as governing and decision-making, received less attention than their other ideas. By some ironic twist of logic in the evolution of ideas, "might has made right." The intellectual gatekeepers have chosen those ideas that support their own power and undermined women's rights to challenge it. Even among those who argued for a value-free social science, many allowed their prejudices to blind them to the bias in their own experiments and observations.

It is sometimes difficult to identify the ideological implications of social science perspectives and to understand why a particular perspective has gained currency in a particular period or through time. In fact, the sociology of knowledge insufficiently examines why some ideas are picked up and developed and others disappear. Gregory Bateson, in his book *Steps to an Ecology of Mind*,[2] asks if there is a process of natural selection that determines the survival of some ideas and the extinction of others. He does not go so far as to suggest the survival of the fittest (what would the fittest ideas be?), but he certainly provokes one to ask why certain ideas survive, who controls their selection, and what purposes their selection serves.

In the competition of ideas, the evolution of the rule of reason has not had many successful advocates where women are concerned. One might ask whether the *number* of advocates influences the survival of an idea. In science the *quality* of an idea is supposed to take precedence over majority rule. Among famous modern philosophers, only John Stuart Mill stands out as a supporter of the equality of women and one who understood causes for their differential behavior. Mill foreshadows the contemporary studies of psychologist Inge Broverman and her associates on the issue of women's dependence, for example. The subjects in the Broverman study, when asked what qualities a "healthy" person would possess, invariably mention self-sufficiency, assertiveness, and self-assurance.[3] These are also the qualities attributed to the healthy male. But the healthy female, according to the common view, possesses the opposite characteristics. The healthy woman, Broverman's study shows, is expected to be dependent and passive. Mill anticipated these findings when he wrote that women were forced by circumstances to act dependent and feel dependent. He provokingly inquired also why what was considered meritorious in a man was considered a vice in a woman. It took Robert K. Merton to identify the basis for this seeming hypocrisy in a sociological phenomenon linked to the maintenance of group boundaries.[4] It is part of what he termed "the self-fulfilling prophecy," in which the behavior practiced and emulated as virtuous by members of the in-group is regarded as inappropriate and wrong when practiced by members of the out-group. Thus, he pointed out, Abe Lincoln is thrifty, while Abe Cohen or Abe Kurasawa is a penny-pincher. This, of course, puts the outsider in an impossible situation. Out-group members are damned if they do, as well as if they don't, because, practiced by them, valued behavior acquires a negative cast. Mill recognized what modern sociologists missed until the 1970s—how the phenomenon applied to women—that biases prevented the formulation of objective descriptions of women's activities and motivations because it made groups of men, especially those in power, more cohesive and made them feel superior by comparison. My research on women lawyers has provided many examples of incidences where in-group virtues became out-group vices. When male trial lawyers display anger in the courtroom, their style is considered dramatic, but when women lawyers do, they are considered abrasive. When women strive for success they are said to be adopting "male values" and to be engaged in deviant behavior.[5] Much earlier, Mill discounted the notion that characteristics attributed to women, such as unselfishness and restraint, were "their nature," again, in the manner of contemporary sociologists, emphasizing a person's situation. Until and through the time of Talcott Parsons, most sociologists still rested their case with Aristotle and Rousseau. And only a few dissenting voices were heard until the late 1960s when Betty Friedan's *The Feminine Mystique*[6]—significantly a popular book, not a sociological tract—first incisively critiqued Parsons' view that it was functional for women to be in the home because their competing presence in the workplace might cause family disruption and disharmony.[7]

Sociologists well through the middle of this century echoed the Rousseauian claim that "women, while intuitive and equipped with a talent for detail are deficient in rationality and quite incapable of abstract thought."[8] Thus the employment of women as clerical workers and their nonpaying employment as housekeepers were ascribed to an innate interest and preference, rather than to a repressive social system which prevented further and higher ambition and, indeed, nipped any ambition in the bud.

Not only were the traits and characteristics of women so conceptualized as to reinforce their state of subordination and therefore legitimate male authority, studies in the social sciences often ignored them altogether. In 1974, I surveyed the field of sociology for consequences of this "male" bias for a special symposium on "Masculine Blinders in the Social Sciences."[9] There, I drew upon the research of Alice Rossi, who suggested that the omission of women from social science investigation stemmed from basic analytical problems in the very structure of the social sciences.[10] Commenting on the lack of serious attention Simone de Beauvoir's The Second Sex[11] received when it first appeared in the 1950s, Rossi suggested that de Beauvoir's eclectic interdisciplinary approach was at odds with the narrow specialization characteristic of the social sciences at that time. Rossi observed:

> Such human characteristics as age and sex play havoc with the specialization that had the academic disciplines in its grip during the 1940s and 1950s with the result that researchers often simply confined their attention to one particular age group and dropped women from their research altogether. Thus a typical sample of subjects in psychology or sociology for more than a decade consisted of young college-age males . . . [therefore] in academic circles the very strength that flowed from its [The Second Sex's] broad synthesizing framework was criticized as a weakness: since no one, the view went, could be a specialist in so many areas, the work was therefore suspect.[12]

Specialists generally ignored women, and only social scientists who went beyond the narrow view considered them subjects worthy of analysis.

Sociological methods have not been specifically deficient with regard to women, but they are generally deficient in failing to question the gaps in our knowledge about any group except the dominant one, whether women, minorities, the elderly, or children.

The methodological and theoretical perspectives offered in ethno-methodology, structural-functional analysis (with its focus on systemic analysis), conflict analysis and other sociological approaches are not intrinsically unsuited for analyzing women in society. Rather, the problem has been that most social scientists of diverse conceptual persuasions have not considered women to be important or interesting subjects of study. The few who have focused on women note the omission of others, not any theoretical or methodological difficulties.[13]

Methods vary, of course, in their specificity and precision. None give a formula for a holistic description and analysis of social groups and processes. The discipline of sociology suffers from lack of theoretical and methodological consensus. This lack of agreement affects the analysis of women as it affects the entire field.

As Rossi suggested, analysis may be so specialized that the whole is lost, or certain important parts of the whole may not come to the sociologist's attention. This is partly a question of values and of fashions. Not only was it traditionally unfashionable for sociologists to study women, but women sociologists were often warned against choosing research topics dealing with women because it was not considered a path to professional success. There is evidence that it was hard to get such research funded[14] and also hard to interest professors in supervising Ph.D. dissertations in this field.[15] Funds are now more available and dissertations have proliferated, but bias prevails. Though male sociologists have never been criticized for studying men in social life, even today male gatekeepers complain of the narrowness of women sociologists specializing in studies of women.

To reach back again in history, the value problem was exacerbated, for younger researchers, those most likely to consider new paradigms because they are not tied to "establishment" research,[16] were not convinced either that women were a group worthy of attention. The more radical among them (who might have been more sensitive to the position of an unpopular underclass than the established sociologists) felt the problems of the poor and the blacks were more pressing. Few, if any, of them saw women as an equally disadvantaged group. Only since women sociologists have gained legitimation, visibility, and resources and have turned their attention to women themselves, has a new scholarship emerged.

The fashions too have changed on some fronts. Women became more modish underdogs in the late 1970s. Any radical journal of sociology today contains articles on women. This ideological catching up is more evident in the dissident press, though there have been breakthroughs in the establishment journals as well.

However, the new scholarship on women is only trickling into the mainstream of sociological knowledge. It is still predominantly women who attend and present papers at sessions on sex roles, or women and work, at professional meetings. The new scholarship is reported in special issues of journals devoted wholly to scholarship by women and is ignored by most male scholars.

* * *

The preceding section has dealt with the sociology of sociology, past and contemporary. I shall now turn to a consideration of how some of the scholarly work concerned with women's issues has reshaped sociological thinking or *should* or *could* reshape it were there the right people to listen to it or read it. I shall select only a sampling—those issues I find intellectually exciting and those I have worked with over the past decade.

I. Socialization

The early socialization model is an important framework in the social sciences. It has had an important influence on our understanding (or lack of understanding) of women as well as of human development. In past work[17] I have argued against the assumption that personality is decisively formed early in life and is thereafter relatively unmalleable. This assumption has blinded us to the impact of socialization after early childhood and of social control systems throughout the life cycle. Early socialization theory is a static rather than a processual model and has prevented sociologists from measuring the extent to which both sexes undergo changes in personality when the conditions of their lives change, that is to say, under new *structural* conditions. The model assumes that whether a person will have a positive or negative self-image, self-confidence, aspiration and motivation depends on what happens in the first decade, or the first six years, or the first eighteen months of his or her life. This set of assumptions has had particularly negative consequences for women and minorities but has also seriously affected acquisition of knowledge about human capacities and impeded work on policy. If we believe capabilities and motivations are determined early, we give up trying to teach and transform people later; nor do we make opportunities available to them.

But the psychological effects of the women's movement on women has necessitated the creation of completely new assumptions about personality development. In my work on lawyers, business people and politicians,[18] I have found that women changed radically when they began pursuing a profession and even more radically if they were successful. Many who were insecure became confident; the unmotivated became ambitious, and the anxious became calm. The women who were reluctant about battling in the courtroom or negotiating contracts found their stage fright disappeared once they actually did the things they had previously felt they couldn't do or would hate doing. Women who were shy found they loved performing in public; women who thought they didn't care much about money wanted to earn the same incomes as men did as a symbol that they had arrived in the professional world. Other social scientists have come to similar conclusions. Melvin Kohn, Carmi Schooler, Jeylan Mortimer,[19] and others have studied the effects of occupation on personality and found that when people perform complex and interesting work, they develop such personality characteristics as autonomy and self-confidence. Boring work makes them insecure and fastidious about details. This research design indicates that conditioning on the job, rather than self-selection into complex jobs, accounts for the correlation with autonomous character traits.

The impact of social structure on personality and behavior has been identified by sociologists for years, but selectively. Using Merton and Goffman's frameworks, I showed in *Woman's Place*[20] that since women in professions did not share men's sex status, they were regarded as deviants and so reacted as deviants. These women felt compelled to "prove" themselves by working too hard or too long, or else learned to retreat and to prefer the unobtrusive backroom, backstage positions they had to take. I tried to show that it was women's positions that caused these reactive behaviors, not "natural" tendencies, preformed personality variables, or early socialization. Rosabeth Kanter's study *Men and Women of the Corporation*[21] made a further impact, indeed became famous, by showing that women locked into dead-end, deadening jobs in the corporation engaged in behavior regarded as petty or narrow. This was not because the women were petty and doted on details: men locked into similar positions behaved in ways pejoratively identified as "like women." Kanter established that differences in behavior in corporations depended on the powerlessness or control of an individual's situation. These were important lessons to be learned by those chronicling social behavior and attitudes.

II. Political Sociology

The nature of political behavior is another sociological issue in which women have been ignored. Descriptions of political processes have ignored the role of women, and political sociologists have assumed that women were not "political animals" by preference and character. Limits on women entering political elites, explained Robert Lane and Seymour Martin Lipset among other political scientists, were due to their involvement in family activities or sex-role socialization which made them more "service oriented" than ambitious.[22] But to ignore the millions of women who engage actively in political campaigns every year, *in the same numbers as men*, is to ignore the grass roots nature of political behavior, the popular basis of all political support, and the uniquely American political process. A paper on women in politics[23] published recently compiled studies showing that, where women's political activity is not squelched by men (for example, in school board elections in which there is little power brokering), family obligations are no impediments either. Even married women with small children were more active than men in these political activities. A recent paper by Carroll[24] shows clearly that rewards rather than participation differs. Marilyn Gittell has also noted that by conceptualizing electoral politics as the sole arena of political behavior, political scientists offer incomplete and inaccurate analysis of political processes,[25] excluding the vast political activity played out in voluntary organizations such as the League of Women Voters, consumer groups, community action groups, and other organizations with large memberships of active women currently and in the past. We need only consider women's participation and leadership in the suffrage movement, the temperance movement, and the benevolent organizations that flourished in the cities during the nineteenth century.[26] In my synthesis of research on political behavior,[27] I challenge theories of political socialization indicating that women are influenced by men, children by parents. I found that sometimes women vote differently but when they vote the same as their husbands and fathers it may be because they have independently arrived at those political beliefs. Indeed, there is evidence that women may even influence their husbands' political choices. Furthermore, some studies show that a child's mother often influences his or her political beliefs when she differs from her husband, and that a child may even influence parents' choices (anyone who lived through the sixties has probably observed this). Looking at all women together and all men together often obscures the independent effects of education and income which might account for differences attributed to a person's gender. Carroll also found women's motives for political participation were the same as men's, although, looking at the *same data,* political scientists interpreted their motives differently.

Attributing stereotyped motivations to women's behavior also undermines their impact as political actors in social movements. Marcia Millman, in an essay whose title, "She Did it All for Love,"[28] characterizes this stereotype, shows how the sociology of deviance largely ignored women. Even when their activity was noticed, it was explained as motivated by emotional attachment to a male deviant. These assumptions also imply that women are less prone to deviance and thus more conventional than men. They therefore fail to take into account deviant behavior which is not criminal and neglect to observe women's influence on changing social norms. Recently, Richard Cloward and Frances Fox Piven,[29] like Millman, show that the category of the deviant should be expanded to include the self-directed and private kinds of deviance women engage in, and the way it is structured by powerful interests such as the mental health industry. Also, they argue that sociologists and lay people alike have assumed, often incorrectly, that women did not and would not engage in collective forms of resistance.

III. Stratification

The field of stratification has neglected the contributions

women have made in understanding the class structure and the place of the family in the class structure. Earlier sociologists merely determined a family's class position by the occupation and income of the male. This concealed the contribution of women's labor-force participation to the position and orientation of the typical middle class American. Analysis of the economic behavior, consumer behavior, education, and reference-group behavior and prestige of middle class families built on two-person incomes has still not been fully analyzed. Sociologists are better at it than many economists. Peter Rossi (et al.) has noted that families' social standing derives from both the husband's and the wife's occupation (though, of course, more the husband's than the wife's).[30] If it had not been for women economists like Cynthia Lloyd and Beth Niemi,[31] who pieced together strands and shards of data, we might still believe women have little commitment to the work force. We would not know that the growing proportion of women in the labor force is due, not only to a dramatic increase in the number of women entering it, but also to a decrease in women withdrawing from it, with the greatest growth among mothers with small children. We must analyse the implications of such hard facts for traditional assumptions about women's priorities and labor force behavior.

I shall now turn to some general sociological concepts which have obstructed objective analysis of sex roles. The dichotomous concepts of "instrumental and expressive" introduced by Talcott Parsons some decades ago, and the notion of "inner and outer worlds" put forth by Erik Erikson, left a lingering lineage of sex-typed conceptual camps. Erikson argued that what women did was "inner," and what men did was "outer,"[32] and Parsons regarded women's behavior as "expressive" and men's as "instrumental,"[33] a spiritual and practical division of labor. The dichotomy of "public and private" as independent realms also flowed from these lines of reasoning and was picked up even by feminist anthropologists.[34] These hypotheses—that women were indeed the emotional actors in the family in most societies, as men were the instrumental actors in the occupational sphere—failed to exercise *both* instrumental and expressive qualities. It further failed to recognize the important interplay and interdependence between institutions. Furthermore, it created blinders to women's economic productivity in the home, on the farm,[35] and in the workplace, sometimes confusing the site with the fact of economic productivity: only if it was away from the home could it be economic activity. The Parsons approach also neglected the way the home was incorporated into the workplace and into organizations—consider, for example, the mill girls of Lowell, Massachusetts, who lived in factory quarters under supervision. Homes were also workplaces when they became boarding houses, and there were many of them at the turn of the century. A family unit, whether headed by male or female, could not maintain itself comfortably without the additional income provided by boarders. For example, more than forty percent of the families in Homestead, Pennsylvania had one or more lodgers at the turn of the century.[37] By the end of the nineteenth century, whole families worked together.

The concepts of Parsons and Erikson were clearly class-bound analyses of suburban, middle class behavior but even then, conceptualized *work* done in the home as *non* work, non-task-goal oriented, and unrelated to the economically [sic] productive workplace. It has taken the emphasis of some economists on human-capital theory to show (insufficiently) how wives' educations actually contribute to their husbands' incomes.[38] Gaye Tuchman has also pointed out that there is a "family" dimension to many work settings. She indicates this is so common it is depicted in the media in such programs as the *Mary Tyler Moore* show and *MASH*.[39]

Parsons and others who shared the conception of the dichotomous behavior of men and women also ignored how emotional male behavior and how instrumental female behavior were in the home and in other institutions, because men were, by definition, the unemotional sex. For Parsons, and for Max Weber before him, the social sciences were at a pre-Pareto state of perception, in which human behavior, that is, male behavior, was viewed as essentially rational. Even in institutions labeled "rational," social behavior always has both rational and irrational elements.[40]

A counter-model to both Parsons and Weber was offered by Habermas,[41] who elaborated on Marcuse's theory that there is a political set of assumptions underlying the notion of "rationality." This counter-model could be extended to sociologists' concept of rationality and instrumentality in major institutions. The assumption that men, but not women, are rational and instrumental has clearly had political ramifications: it has provided a

theortical rationalization for the perpetuation of male domination. Arlie Hochschild,[42] whose feminist perspective has led her
to consider why sociologists have not developed a sociology of
feeling and emotion, has opened an interesting and important
line of analysis on how emotions are socially structured and how
people manipulate their own emotions to conform with social
norms. She shows how what has been thought to be *un*conscious
behavior, e.g. the emotions, may in fact be very conscious,
opening up an entire subfield of exploration in the interface
between sociology and psychology.

The failure of sociology to deal meaningfully with the place of
women in society throws a harsh light on the theoretical models
that have shaped the profession for the past quarter-century. It
is time new models were proposed or the old ones altered to
provide an image of society less distant from reality. Events have
made our sensitivities more acute and have enabled us to better
understand the limitations of our theories and methods.
Theoretical and methodological work that was free of
stereotypes would provide us with new insights, not only into the
sociology of women's place in society, but into the sociological
profile of all society, and of all social systems.

NOTES

1. Princeton, N.J.: Princeton University Press, 1979.
2. New York: Ballentine Books, 1972.
3. I. K. Broverman, et al., "Sex Role Stereotypes and Clinical Judgements of Mental Health," *Journal of Consulting and Clinical Psychology*, vol. 34 (1970) pp. 1–7.
4. Merton, "Self-Fulfilling Prophecy" in *Social Theory and Social Structure* (Glencoe, Illinois: The Free Press, 1957).
5. I discuss these processes in more detail in a chapter, "Outsiders Within" in *Women in Law* (New York: Basic Books, 1981).
6. Betty Friedan, *The Feminine Mystique* (New York: Norton, 1963).
7. Talcott Parsons, "Age and Sex in the Social Structure of the U.S." in *Essays in Sociological Theory* (Glencoe, Ill.: Free Press, 1954).
8. Susan Moller Okin, *Women in Western Political Thought* (Princeton University Press, 1979), p. 100.
9. "A Different Angle of Vision: Notes on the Selective Eye of Sociology," *Social Science Quarterly*, December 1974, pp. 654–56. Segments of that analysis are incorporated in this paper.
10. Alice Rossi, *The Feminist Papers: From Adams to Beauvoir* (New York: Columbia University Press, 1973).

11. Simone de Beauvoir, *The Second Sex* (New York: Knopf, 1952; originally published in France by Librarie Gallimard, 1949).
12. Rossi, *Feminist Papers*, p. 673.
13. For example, Shulamith Firestone, *The Dialectic of Sex: The Case for Feminist Revolution* (New York: Morrow, 1970) and Juliet Mitchell, *Woman's Estate* (New York: Pantheon Books, 1971) both have examined women's roles within society from a Marxist perspective; Rose Laub Coser and Gerald Rukoff, "Women in the Occupational World: Social Disruption and Conflict," *Social Problems*, 18 (Spring 1971), pp. 535–54, and I have used role theory and a functional analysis perspective and exchange theory; Arlene Daniels used a sociology of knowledge perspective in "Feminist Perspectives in Sociological Research," in Millman and Kanter, eds., *Another Voice* (New York: Doubleday, 1975).
14. James McCartney, "Effect of Financial Support on Growth of Sociological Specialties," in E. Tiryakian, ed., *The Phenomenon of Sociology* (New York: Appleton Century Crofts, 1971), p. 395, showed that only 26.7 percent of articles on family research (that area where most sociological work on women has been done) show grant support, as opposed to 70 percent in the sociology of education, 66 percent in the sociology of medicine, and 13 other fields which also indicate higher support.
15. It seems only fair to report this was not my personal experience at Columbia University in the 1960s where both William J. Goode and Robert K. Merton offered support and enthusiasm for my dissertation on women professionals.
16. Thomas Kuhn, *The Structure of Scientific Revolution* (2nd ed., Chicago: University of Chicago Press, 1970).
17. "Separate and Unequal: Notes on Women's Achievement", *Social Policy* vol. 6, No. 5 March/April 1976 pp. 17–23, p. 21.
18. See *Women in Law* (New York: Basic Books, 1981), "Women and Power: The Roles of Women in Politics in the United States," in Epstein and Coser, eds., *Access to Power: Cross-National Studies on Women and Elites* (London: George Allen and Unwin, 1981), pp. 124–46; and "Institutional Barriers: What Keeps Women Out of the Executive Suite?" in F. Gordon and M. Strober, eds., *Bringing Women into Management* (New York: McGraw-Hill, 1975) pp. 7–20.
19. Melvin Kohn and Cami Schooler, "Occupational Experience and Psychological Functioning: An Assessment of Reciprocal Effects," *American Sociological Review* (February 1973) pp. 97–118. Also Mortimer and Jon Lawrence, "Work Experience and Occupational Value Socialization: A Longitudinal Study," *American Journal of Sociology* vol. 84, no. 6 (May 1979) pp. 1361–85.
20. Berkeley, Los Angeles, London: University of California Press, 1970.
21. New York: Basic Books, 1977.
22. Cynthia Fuchs Epstein, "Women and Power: The Roles of Women in Politics in the United States," in Cynthia Fuchs Epstein and Rose Laub Coser, eds., *Access to Power* (London: George Allen and Unwin, 1981).
23. Ibid.
24. Berenice A. Carroll, "Political Science, Part I: American Politics and Political Behavior," *Signs*, vol. 5, no. 2 (1979) p. 289.
25. Marilyn Gittell and Teresa Shtob, "Changing Women's Roles in Political Volunteerism and Reform of the City," *Signs*, vol. 5, no. 3 (Spring 1980), pp. 567–78.

162

26. Gaye Tuchman, "Betwixt Public and Private: Unintended Affirmation of Ideology," (unpublished paper, Spring 1981).
27. "Women and Power: The Roles of Women in Politics in the United States," in Cynthia Fuchs Epstein and Rose Laub Coser, eds., *Access to Power* (London: George Allen and Unwin, 1981).
28. Marcia Millman, "She Did It All for Love," in Marcia Millman and Rosabeth Kanter, eds., *Another Voice* (New York: Doubleday, 1975).
29. Richard C. Cloward and Frances Fox Piven, "Hidden Protest: The Channeling of Female Innovation and Resistance," *Signs* (Summer, 1979) vol. 4, no. 4, pp. 651-69.
30. Peter Rossi, et al., "Measuring Household Social Standing," *Social Science Research* 3 (1974) pp. 1969-90.
31. Cynthia Lloyd and Beth Niemi, *The Economics of Sex Differentials* (New York: Columbia University Press, 1979) chapter II.
32. Erik H. Erikson, *Childhood and Society* (2nd ed; New York: Norton, 1963) pp. 230-31.
33. Talcott Parsons, "Age and Sex in the Social Structure of the United States" in *Essays in Sociological Theory* (Revised ed.; Glencoe, Illinois: The Free Press, 1954) pp. 89-103.
34. Michelle Zimbalist Rosaldo and Louise Lamphere, eds., *Woman, Culture, and Society* (Stanford, California: Stanford University Press, 1974).
35. See Elise Boulding, "The Labor of U.S. Farm Women: A Knowledge Gap" in *Sociology of Work and Occupations* vol. 7, no. 31 (August 1980) pp. 261-91.
36. Alice Kessler Harris, *Women Have Always Worked* (Old Westbury, New York: The Feminist Press, 1981) p. 57.
37. Ibid.
38. See Beth T. Niemi and Harriet Zellner, "Intra-Family Human Capital Transfer" *Atlantic Economic Journal* vol. 8, no. 1 (March 1980) p. 71.
39. Gaye Tuchman, "Betwixt Public and Private: Unintended Affirmation of Ideology," (unpublished paper, Spring 1981).
40. Raymond Firth, *Primitive Polynesian Economy* (London: Routledge and Kegan Paul, 1939) points out the rational elements of the ritual associated with the launching of canoes by the Tikopia.
41. Jürgen Habermas, *Toward a Rational Society* (Boston: Beacon Press, 1970).
42. Arlie Russell Hochschild, "The Sociology of Feeling and Emotion," in Millman and Kanter, eds., *Another Voice* (New York: Doubleday, 1975) and "Emotion Work, Feeling Rules, and the Social Structure," in *American Journal of Sociology* vol. 85, no. 3 (November 1979) pp. 551-76.